Short Bike Rides™

in and around

New York City

Help Us Keep This Guide Up to Date

Every effort has been made by the authors and editors to make this guide as accurate and useful as possible. However, many things can change after a guide is published—establishments close, phone numbers change, facilities come under new management, etc.

We would love to hear from you concerning your experiences with this guide and how you feel it could be made better and be kept up to date. While we may not be able to respond to all comments and suggestions, we'll take them to heart, and we'll also make certain to share them with the authors. Please send your comments and suggestions to the following address:

The Globe Pequot Press
Reader Response/Editorial Department
P.O. Box 480
Guilford, CT 06437

Or you may e-mail us at:

editorial@globe-pequot.com

Thanks for your input, and happy travels!

Short Bike Rides™ Series

Short Bike Rides™
in and around
New York City

Third Edition

Phil and Wendy Harrington

The Globe Pequot Press

Guilford, Connecticut

Short Bike Rides is a trademark of The Globe Pequot Press.

Cover design by Saralyn D'Amato-Twomey
Cover photo by Chris Dubé

Library of Congress Cataloging-in-Publication Data
Harrington, Phil.
    Short bike rides in and around New York City / Phil and Wendy
        Harrington.—3rd ed.
            p.   cm. — (Short bike rides series)
        ISBN 0-7627-0333-4
        1. Bicycle touring—New York Metropolitan Area—Guidebooks.   2. New
    York Metropolitan Area—Guidebooks.   I. Harrington, Wendy.   II. Title.
    III. Series.
GV1045.5.N72N494   1999
796.6'4'097471—dc21   98-31866
                                                                                                            CIP

✪ This text is printed on recycled paper.
Manufactured in the United States of America
Third Edition/Third Printing

To our beloved daughter, Helen

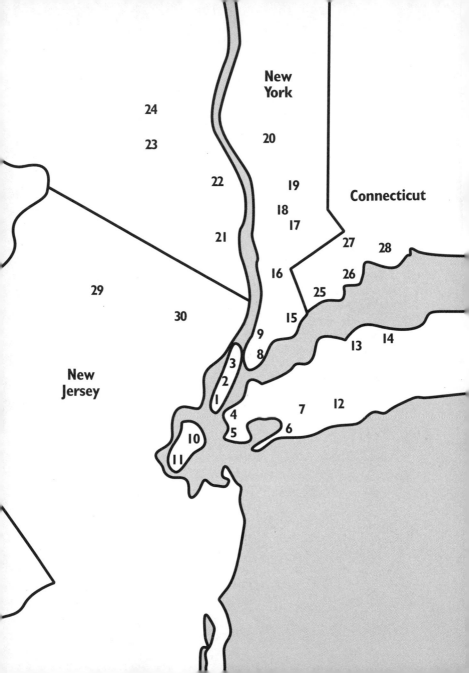

Contents

Connecticut

New Jersey

Appendixes

Acknowledgments

One of the most rewarding aspects of researching and writing this book has been the many helpful people we have dealt with along the way. Every agency we contacted gladly provided information and details. Were it not for their help, the quality of this book would have suffered greatly.

Though we cannot possibly name everyone who has aided us, throughout the two years it took to assemble this work, we would like to single out a few folks who have been especially helpful:

Elizabeth Fenton, Darien Historical Society

Eric Hilton

Pamela Hurst, Rockland Economic Development Corporation

Clif Kranish, New York Cycle Club

Anne McClellan, Neighborhood Open Space Coalition

Carol Ortner, Alley Pond Environmental Center

Gordon Rabeler, Rockland Economic Development Corporation

Karen Sposato, Westchester County Public Information Office

To them, and to everyone who contributed to this work in one way or another, we extend our heartfelt thanks.

—Phil and Wendy Harrington
Smithtown, New York

Overview of the Rides

	Adult	Family (bike path)	Challenging
1 The Battery to the Village	●		
2 Central Park	●	●	
3 Upper Upper West Side	●	●[1]	
4 A Two-Borough Tour	●		
5 Brooklyn Greenway	●	●[2]	
6 Jamaica Bay Roundabout	●	●[3]	
7 Queens Greenway	●	●[4]	
8 Van Cortlandt Park to Pelham Bay Park	●	●[5]	
9 Riverdale, Spuyten Duyvil, and Kingsbridge	●		●
10 Grymes Hill to Snug Harbor	●	●[6]	●
11 Great Kills to South Beach and Todt Hill	●	●[7]	
12 Bethpage Bikeway and Beyond	●	●	
13 Greenlawn–Huntington	●	●[8]	
14 Smithtown	●	●[9]	●
15 Harrison to Rye	●		
16 Kensico Reservoir Loop	●	●[10]	●
17 Bedford and Vicinity	●		●
18 Katonah and Croton Reservoir	●		●
19 Titicus Reservoir Quickie	●	●[11]	●
20 The Putnam Panic!	●		●
21 Hudson River Loop	●	●[12]	●
22 Stony Point	●	●[13]	●
23 Monroe to Chester	●		
24 Goshen to Washingtonville	●		
25 Greenwich	●	●[14]	
26 Darien	●		
27 New Canaan	●		
28 Fairfield Pizza Loop	●		
29 Lake Hopatcong	●		●
30 Harrington Park and Vicinity	●		

1. Family portion (bike paths) restricted to Riverside Park.
2. Family portion (bike paths) restricted to Prospect Park and along Belt Parkway.
3. Family portion along Cross Bay Boulevard, inside Floyd Benett Field, and along Belt Parkway bikeway.
4. Family portion (bike paths) restricted to parks as noted in text.
5. Family portion (bike path) restricted to Van Cortlandt Park and Pelham Bay Park.
6. Family portion restricted to within Clove Lakes Park and Silver Lake.
7. Family portion restricted to within Great Kills Park.

Off-Road	Cityscape	County Roads	Coastal	
	•			1
	•			2
	•			3
	•		•	4
	•		•	5
	•		•	6
	•		•	7
	•		•	8
				9
	•	•		10
		•		11
		•		12
		•	•	13
		•	•	14
		•	•	15
		•		16
•		•		17
		•		18
		•		19
		•		20
				21
		•		22
		•		23
		•		24
		•		25
		•	•	26
		•		27
		•		28
		•	•	29
		•		30

8. Family portion restricted to within residential area around Woodland Road.
9. Family portion restricted to paths within Sunken Meadow State Park and Blydenburgh County Park.
10. Family portion restricted to paths within Kensico Dam Plaza.
11. Family portion restricted to paths in Ward Pound Ridge Reservation.
12. Family portion of ride within Blauvelt Park.
13. Family portion of ride within Bear Mountain State Park.
14. Family portion of ride within Bruce Park.

Introduction

Most people wouldn't think of using the words "bicycling" and "New York City" in the same sentence. After all, New York has the reputation of being one huge traffic snarl complicated by potholes, irate cabbies, double-parked cars, and death-defying drivers, in-line skaters, and pedestrians darting about. While this may be true some of the time in some parts of the city, at other times, and in other parts, New York can take on the serenity of a small town. Indeed, the city offers a wide and varied environment for the bike rider. Nowhere else in the world can two such divergent themes be so successfully combined as in New York City. The urban cyclist just has to be a little clever.

In this book, we take you, the reader and cyclist, on a bike tour of the five boroughs of New York City. City cycling is like nothing you have ever experienced before! It is both exhilarating and relaxing at the same time—a true dichotomy. You will enjoy it.

Likewise, the countryside around New York City offers a tremendous range of settings for the cyclist. Within an hour's drive, you will find everything from long, flat beachfront expanses that appeal to the casual rider, to hilly terrain that will test the most seasoned biker. Whether you are an urbanite seeking escape or a suburbanite seeking adventure, you will find what you are looking for.

Be it urban, suburban, or rural, each route has been chosen based on several criteria, such as the amount of traffic, road surface quality, terrain, scenic beauty, historical significance, and general interest. We hope you will get a chance to try each.

We have provided directions to the beginning of the ride from a nearby major highway or thoroughfare. Of course, it is not always practical or possible for all readers to travel to the starting points by automobile. With this in mind, we have tried to list alternative methods of getting to the starting point by public transportation. If you're a subway cyclist, you ought to check our advice, listed below under "Mass Transit."

You will notice that many of the routes can be joined to form longer journeys. In some cases, two rides share some common roads, while others may be linked by short connectors.

We have tried to make the accompanying maps as complete as and informative as possible. Along with street names and attractions, they include the suggested direction of travel, location of larger hills ("+" for uphill, "-" for downhill), rest stops, and possible shortcuts. We have also designated routes for optional side trips—described in the text—with bold dashed lines on the maps. Dashed lines are used to show connections with other bike routes as well.

A Few Tips and Suggestions

Bikes. Nowadays, most cyclists prefer to use multispeed bicycles. They come in a variety of shapes and sizes, but the favorite today seems to be the mountain bicycle. The mountain bike features thick, knobby tires, a reinforced frame, straight handlebars, and a cushioning saddle. Most are equipped with advanced hand-brake systems and 18- to 24-speed gearing. While other bikes should confine their travel to either paved or hard-packed dirt roads, mountain bikes are sturdy enough to blaze their own trails. It is because of their ruggedness that mountain bikes are especially popular among city dwellers. They are better suited to put up with the abuse of bumps and holes than their more fragile cousins.

Still, many cyclists prefer a "racing-style" bicycle. These bikes are characterized by their light weight, downturned handlebars, skinny saddles, and even skinnier tires. Actually, labeling all bikes of this genre as "racers" is a misnomer. Most are either "touring" bikes or "road" bikes. Regardless of the name, this style of bicycle is excellent for touring most suburban and country thoroughfares. If you are thinking of going on long excursions (30 miles or more), a road bike is probably your best choice, thanks to its lighter weight, more aerodynamic profile, and lower road resistance of its high-pressure tires.

A third type of bicycle whose popularity is growing fast is the "hybrid." As the name implies, it takes features from both the mountain bike (upright handlebars, cushiony seat, and frame geometry) and the road bike (light weight, thin tires) and combines them into one vehicle. Many cyclists believe that hybrids are the best all-around bikes.

Helmets. The single most important accessory you can buy is a cycling helmet. Not convinced? Once we were riding along a quiet road on Long Island when, while going down a steep hill and around a sharp curve, one of your authors met a pothole about 3 feet wide and 9 inches deep. The pothole won the fight and Phil went flying, only to meet the road head-on! Were it not for his helmet, he surely would have suffered a concussion or skull fracture (he ended up with only minor whiplash, though his left leg was a bit mangled)! 'Nuff said— get a helmet and make sure it meets either ANSI or Snell criteria (two testing organizations).

Locks. Your bicycle is hot property in and around New York City, and there are those who want to take it from you. While there is no absolute way to prevent theft, the best deterrent is to get the strongest U-shaped lock you can find. Secure both wheels and the frame to something that will prevent the thief from slipping the lock and bike over it (a permanent bike rack, street sign, or double parking meter are the best).

Some lock manufacturers offer up to a $1000 anti-theft guarantee for one year after purchase. These policies are *not* unconditional, however. Most, for instance, offer worldwide coverage *except in New York City,* so shop around.

Safety. The law of the land requires cyclists to follow all rules applicable to cars. This includes obeying all traffic lights and signs, using hand signals when turning, and riding on the right hand side of the road (with traffic, not against it).

In this day and age, violent crime can happen anywhere. That's why we recommend that you always ride with a companion—there is safety in numbers.

Tools. Besides a friend, be sure to bring along spare parts and tools in case an emergency repair is needed. Here's a list of the most commonly needed items:

> Spare tube (bring two)
> Tire-repair kit (patch kit, tire irons, etc.)

Hand pump
Air-pressure gauge
Wrenches for adjusting the seat or handlebars
First-aid kit

Sure, they add some weight but we would rather carry a few extra pounds than be left stranded in the middle of nowhere.

Mass Transit. Getting around in and out of the city is often far easier by using mass transit than by driving in a car. With that in mind, here is some information on traveling on mass transit with your bicycle.

Subways. The Metropolitan Transportation Authority allows bicycles on New York City subways at all times, but they request that you be considerate toward other passengers. With that in mind, the MTA offers the following guidelines:

1. Avoid crowded stations and trains. "Lettered" trains (that is, the IND lines) have bigger stations and roomier subway cars. If possible, choose express trains since they have fewer stops and less boarding and exiting.

2. Enter and exit through the station service gate. Deposit your token or use your MetroCard, roll the turnstile, and enter through the service gate. Don't try to lift your bicycle over the turnstile or try to carry it through a "high-wheel" revolving entrance or exit.

3. Board train after exiting passengers have detrained.

4. Stay near either end of the subway car.

5. Stand by your bicycle when on the subway, moving it when others need to get by.

6. Carry your bicycle up and down stairways.

7. Follow instructions from transit police and station and train personnel.

Trains. For getting out to the suburbs, you can't beat a train trip. The MTA, which runs both the Metro-North and Long Island Railroad lines, requires that cyclists obtain a permit before boarding a train. In 1998, permits for the Harlem, Hudson, and New Haven lines of Metro-North could be purchased for $5.00 at Grand Central Station, while those for the Long Island Railroad's many branches could be obtained for $5.00 at Penn Station. In both cases, bicycles are not allowed on board during weekday rush hours (call for times for your station) and on the following holidays: New Years Eve and Day, Mothers Day, Saint Patrick's Day, Rosh Hashana Eve, Yom Kippur Eve, Thanksgiving Eve and Day, and Christmas Eve and Day. Bikes are permitted at all times on weekends, except when one of the holidays listed above occurs on a Saturday or Sunday.

The PATH trains to and from New Jersey also require a permit, which may be obtained by calling (800) 234–PATH or (201) 216–6247. Several boarding restrictions must also be observed if you plan on bringing your bike onto a PATH train. Bikes are not allowed on board weekdays from 6:00 to 9:30 A.M. and 3:00 to 6:30 P.M., as well as Saturdays from 1:00 to 7:00 P.M. There are no restrictions on Sundays and holidays.

Finally, New Jersey Transit trains also require a permit, which can be had for free by calling (201) 491–9400, or may be picked up at Penn Station in Manhattan or at Track 10 at the Hoboken, New Jersey, train station. No bicycles are permitted during morning rush hours to New York City or afternoon rush hours to New Jersey.

Buses. Sorry, but bicycles are not allowed on city buses, with the exception of the QBx1, a bus that crosses the Bronx-Whitestone Bridge and is specially outfitted with a bike rack on the front. The QBx1 runs approximately every thirty minutes, but only stops for bikes at two pick-up points. In Queens, catch the bus at the Whitestone Expressway Service Road at 20th Avenue; in the Bronx, at the Hutchinson River Expressway Service Road and Lafayette Avenue. You pay the regular mass-transit fare; your bike rides for free. For additional information, call the Queens Surface Corporation at (718) 445–3100.

Some private bus lines do allow bicycles, including Greyhound (800–231–2222), Short Line (800–631–8405), Adirondack/Pine Hill Trailways (800–858–8555), Peter Pan (800–343–9999), Hampton Jitney (800–936–0440), Academy (212–971–9054), and Bonanza (212-947-1766). All require the bike be boxed and placed in the bus's luggage area; some charge a carrying fee.

Ferries. Finally, bicycles are welcome on the Staten Island Ferry at no charge, although they are restricted to the lower (car) level.

Roads. Every resident of the New York City tri-state area is well aware that road conditions are constantly changing. A smooth, pleasant road today can be transformed into a dug-up construction site tomorrow. That cannot be helped or anticipated. If you have suggestions or comments on how the routes can be modified or improved, however, we eagerly welcome your thoughts. Jot them down and send them to us in care of Globe Pequot Press, P.O. Box 833, Old Saybrook, Connecticut 06475, or via e-mail to pharrington@ compuserve.com. All suggestions will be considered for future editions. We will attempt to acknowledge all correspondence, but in case we miss yours, thanks in advance. And when cycling the Internet, be sure to visit the "Short Bike Rides in and around New York City Home Page" at http://members.aol.com/bikebookny/sbrnyc.htm, where you will find links to a variety of cycling clubs, rides, shops, and other cycling-related sites.

Happy, safe cycling!

Manhattan
The Battery to the Village

Mileage:	5
Terrain:	Flat
Traffic:	Disastrous on weekdays but light on both weekend and holiday mornings.
Facilities:	Rest rooms and water fountain at Battery Park; several small restaurants and food stores in and around Washington Square Park
Things to see:	Battery Park, Lower New York Harbor (including the Statue of Liberty), Castle Clinton National Monument, Eisenhower War Memorial, American Stock Exchange, World Trade Center, Tribeca, Soho, Greenwich Village, Washington Square Park, New York University, City Hall, Trinity Episcopal Church, New York Stock Exchange, Federal Hall National Memorial, Fraunces Tavern

Although this is one of the nation's most hectic areas five days a week, the concrete canyons of Manhattan's financial district take on the eerie emptiness of a ghost town on weekend and holiday mornings. It is at those times that the city's hustle and bustle give way to the quiet serenity of a morning bike ride.

Our trip around lower Manhattan starts in **Battery Park** at the island's southern tip. The site of a fort built in 1624 by the city's first Dutch settlers, the Battery offers commanding views of the lower **New York Harbor** and the **Statue of Liberty**. The park itself has many

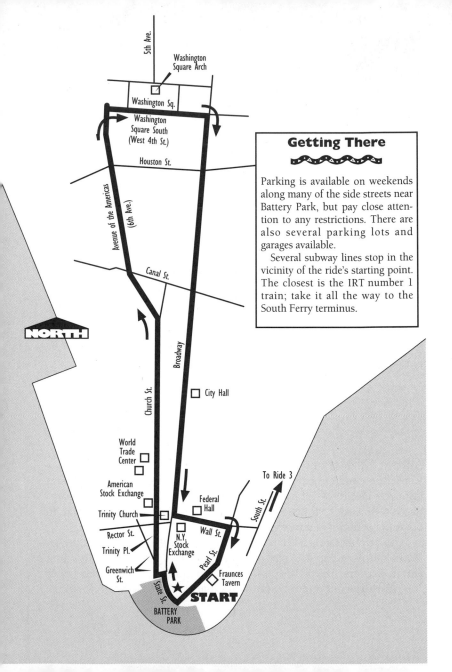

5th Ave.

Washington Square Arch

Washington Sq.

Washington Square South (West 4th St.)

Houston St.

Avenue of the Americas (6th Ave.)

Canal St.

NORTH

Broadway

Church St.

City Hall

World Trade Center

American Stock Exchange

Trinity Church

Rector St.

Trinity Pl.

Greenwich St.

State St.

BATTERY PARK

Federal Hall

N.Y. Stock Exchange

Wall St.

Pearl St.

South St.

Fraunces Tavern

To Ride 3

★ START

Getting There

Parking is available on weekends along many of the side streets near Battery Park, but pay close attention to any restrictions. There are also several parking lots and garages available.

Several subway lines stop in the vicinity of the ride's starting point. The closest is the IRT number 1 train; take it all the way to the South Ferry terminus.

0.0   Begin at corner of State and Pearl Streets, across from Battery Park.

0.1   Left onto Battery Place, then left onto Greenwich Street.

0.3   Veer right onto Trinity Place, which changes names to Church Street at the World Trade Center.

1.2   Left onto the Avenue of the Americas (6th Avenue).

2.2   Right onto Washington Square South (West 4th Street).

2.6   Right at first traffic light after Washington Square Park onto Broadway.

4.3   Left across from Trinity Church onto Wall Street.

4.5   Bear right onto Pearl Street. Take Pearl Street to State Street and Battery Park.

paved sidewalks for a slow (and cautious) tour. Within Battery Park is the **Castle Clinton National Monument.** Built in 1811, it served as army headquarters during the War of 1812 and as a defense outpost to guard the port of New York. Also found within Battery Park is the **Eisenhower War Memorial,** which pays homage to the thousands of U.S. soldiers who died overseas during World War II.

The ride begins at the park's northern perimeter. Head north on Greenwich Street, then veer right onto Trinity Place. About 0.25 mile along you will pass 86 Trinity Place, home of the **American Stock Exchange.** North of this point Trinity Place changes names to Church Street.

As you pass the intersection of Church and Liberty Streets, you will be riding in the shadow of the **World Trade Center,** a sixteen-acre office and plaza complex completed in 1970. Standing next to the twin 110-story towers while straddling a bicycle can certainly make one feel insignificant! If you have never walked through the Trade Center plaza, take the time to do so—but first find a place to lock your bike up securely. (You may use a street sign, but not a parking meter.)

Inside are many renowned retail stores and eateries. If time permits, take the elevator up, up, up to the 107th-floor indoor observation deck or the 110th-floor open promenade that panoramic view from either floor is truly breathtaking.

Back down on the ground, press northward on Church Street, leaving the financial district behind. The route now enters **Tribeca** (named for the *Tri*angle *Be*low *Ca*nal Street) and then **Soho** (the area *So*uth of *Ho*uston Street), two trendy residential areas that also offer many shops, galleries, and restaurants.

Veer left onto the Avenue of the Americas (6th Avenue). At Washington Square South (West 4th Street) turn right. You are now in the heart of **Greenwich Village**, well known for its bookstores, boutiques, and art galleries. A short side trip along Greenwich Avenue will reveal many small handicraft, clothing, and jewelry shops (try not to buy too much—remember the trip home).

Pedaling eastward along Washington Square South, the route traverses the southern perimeter of **Washington Square Park**. At the head of the square stands the mighty Washington Arch, designed by Stanford White. The park hosts an ongoing three-season festival, with art shows and informal folk and jazz concerts found here throughout the spring, summer, and fall. Surrounding the park is the campus of **New York University**.

Continue east of Washington Square Park to the first traffic light; turn right onto Broadway. As you make your way southward along the lower end of the "Great White Way," you will pass **City Hall** nestled in a pleasant park on the corner of Broadway and Chambers Street.

Farther down Broadway, at the corner of Rector Street, lies **Trinity Episcopal Church**. The original structure on this site was completed by early settlers in 1697 and later served as the first home of King's College in the mid-1700s. (King's College later moved uptown and changed its name to Columbia University.) The present structure was constructed in 1846. Allow enough time to visit the church's museum and to take one of the tours offered weekdays at 2:00 P.M. As you walk around the churchyard, look for the headstones of Alexander Hamilton and Robert Fulton, who are both buried out back.

Leaving the churchyard, cross Broadway and turn left onto Wall

Street, home of the **New York Stock Exchange.** The Stock Exchange is closed on weekends and holidays but open on regular business days with free tours and a visitor's gallery. If you are planning a visit, we suggest that you do so on foot; this is no place for a bicycle!

Farther down Wall Street, pause at the **Federal Hall National Memorial.** Federal Hall served as both the site of George Washington's inauguration on April 30, 1789, and the nation's Capitol until August 1790. Although the present building is just over 100 years old, it houses the original brown slab upon which George Washington stood to take his oath of office.

As you approach the east end of Wall Street, you have a choice to make. To return to Battery Park, turn right onto Pearl Street. If you wish, instead, to link up with Ride #3 (visiting the South Street Seaport, the Brooklyn Bridge, and Brooklyn Heights), continue one block farther to South Street and bear left.

The last stop before the ride's end is at **Fraunces Tavern** at 54 Pearl Street. This was the 1783 site of Washington's farewell to the officers of the Continental Army, as well as the first home of the United States War Department. Today, Fraunces Tavern is a restored museum and restaurant.

From Fraunces Tavern continue along Pearl Street to State Street. There, adjacent to the Staten Island Ferry terminal, is Battery Park, your starting point.

For Further Information

Castle Clinton National Monument (212) 344–7220
World Trade Center Visitors' Information (212) 466–7397
Trinity Episcopal Church (212) 602–0800
New York Stock Exchange (212) 623–5167
Federal Hall National Memorial (212) 264–4367
Fraunces Tavern (212) 425–1776

Manhattan
Central Park

Mileage:	7
Terrain:	Hilly in spots
Traffic:	Virtually no car traffic but on weekends need to take caution with skaters, pedestrians, and other cyclists.
Facilities:	Rest rooms and water fountains located throughout the park; most found around the attractions toward the south end of the park
Things to see:	Tavern on the Green, Sheep Meadow, the Pond, Wollman Memorial Rink, Gotham Miniature Golf Course, the Carousel, the Dairy, Central Park Zoo, Children's Zoo, the Mall, the Bandshell, Bethesda Fountain, the Lake, Cleopatra's Needle, the Great Lawn, the Metropolitan Museum of Art, the Reservoir, Strawberry Fields

As difficult as it is to imagine today, Central Park was little more than swampland and shanties before 1853. That year, New York City acquired the park's first 700 acres—between Fifth and Eighth Avenues and 59th and 106th Streets—for the express purposes of creating what would be the first landscaped public park in the United States. (The park was extended to 110th Street in 1863, bringing it to its current 843 acres.) After holding a contest looking for the best design, the Central Park Commission selected a plan submitted by

Frederick Law Olmsted, the park's commissioner at the time, and Calvert Vaux, an English-born architect. Their scheme called for the creation of an English landscape, with rolling meadows, a formal mall or promenade, and many carriage drives, pedestrian walkways, and equestrian paths. More than forty bridges eliminate the many routes from crossing each other on the same grade.

Today, many of the park roads are shared among pedestrains, horses, in-line skaters, bicyclists, and cars, creating quite a hectic scene at times. Happily, the park roads are closed to automobiles from 10:00 A.M. to 3:00 P.M. on weekdays and all day Saturday and Sunday, with extended hours during the summer.

Although you are free to enter the park at any point, the ride here begins at the West 67th Street entrance. There, on the right, is the world-famous restaurant, **Tavern on the Green**. No doubt some of the patrons would be surprised to learn that the restaurant was originally built to house sheep. In fact, sheep called Central Park home as recently as 1930. The large open field bordering the road to the left is still referred to as **Sheep Meadow**.

Turn right onto West Drive and proceed southward. The road soon veers to the left to become East Drive, heading uptown. Beyond the trees on the right is a horseshoe-shaped body of water simply called the **Pond**. It's a lovely place to pause and soak up a bit of nature. Just beyond the Pond is **Wollman Memorial Rink**. From April to October the rink is outfitted for roller and in-line skating, while ice skaters enjoy the facility during the winter months. Next to the rink is the **Gotham Miniature Golf Course**. Created under the auspices of Donald Trump, the course features a creative setting around scale models of city landmarks. The rink and golf course are open daily with nominal fees for players.

As you approach the 65th Street overpass, don't be surprised if you hear carousel music coming from the left. The **Carousel** was built in 1908 for Coney Island and was later moved to Central Park. Its fifty-eight hand-carved horses continue to delight children today just as they did their great-grandparents almost a century ago.

Across East Drive from the Carousel, look for the **Dairy**, a dark-brown building set among a thicket of trees. Dating back to a time

7

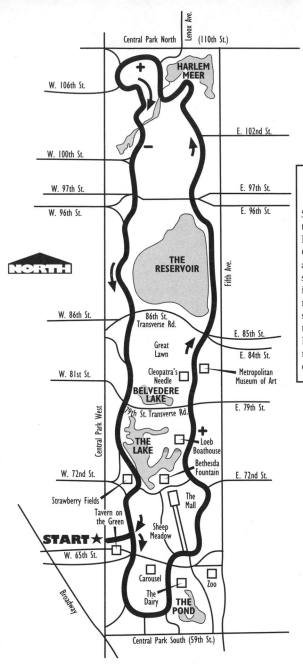

Lenox Ave.

Central Park North (110th St.)

HARLEM MEER

W. 106th St.

E. 102nd St.

W. 100th St.

W. 97th St. E. 97th St.

W. 96th St. E. 96th St.

NORTH

THE RESERVOIR

Fifth Ave.

W. 86th St.

86th St. Transverse Rd.

E. 85th St.

Great Lawn

E. 84th St.

W. 81st St.

Cleopatra's Needle

Metropolitan Museum of Art

BELVEDERE LAKE

E. 79th St.

79th St. Transverse Rd.

Central Park West

THE LAKE

Loeb Boathouse

Bethesda Fountain

W. 72nd St. E. 72nd St.

Strawberry Fields

The Mall

Tavern on the Green

START ★

Sheep Meadow

W. 65th St.

Broadway

Carousel

Zoo

The Dairy

THE POND

Central Park South (59th St.)

Getting There

Several subway lines including the IND A, B, C, and D and the IRT 1, 2, 3, and 9, stop at Columbus Circle (59th Street and Central Park West), just south of the ride's start. Parking is at a premium, though spaces may be found on adjacent streets. For suburbanites, take the train to Grand Central or Penn Station, then proceed northward along one of the avenues to the park.

DIREC-TIONS
at a glance

No specific directions are needed for this ride. Enter the park at West 67th Street (or at one of the park's many other entrances) and proceed to the right along West (or East) Drive on the designated bike lane.

when cows grazed nearby, the Dairy is now home to the park's visitors' center. Inside you will find a wide variety of exhibits, maps, and brochures describing the park's many programs. Be sure to stop in.

The **Central Park Zoo** is another park attraction that is enjoying a rebirth after major renovation. Centrally located in the zoo is the sea lion pool. It is easy to become entranced while watching these playful creatures swim about. Surrounding the pool are exhibit halls highlighting different climates. These range from a frigid arctic setting to a tropical rain forest. As of Fall 1998, the nearby **Children's Zoo** was closed while it underwent major renovation.

Just past the zoo on the left is a 1,212-foot-long promenade called the **Mall**. Its wide walkway is lined with statues of famous authors, including William Shakespeare and Sir Walter Scott, and shaded by two rows of noble elm trees. At the north end of the Mall stands the **Bandshell**, where concerts and performances are held nearly every night during the summer months. Farther along, at the 72nd Street transverse, is the **Bethesda Fountain**. The fountain's link to its biblical namesake, the Bethesda Pool, is made immediately apparent by the statue of an angel in its center.

From the fountain you have a magnificent view of the **Lake**. The Loeb Boathouse, on the Lake's eastern shore, rents bicycles to visitors who want to join in the fun of touring Central Park by pedal power. The boathouse also rents rowboats for use on the Lake. You'll find a restaurant and a snack bar there as well.

As you cross 79th Street, look on the left for **Cleopatra's Needle**, an Egyptian obelisk made of pink granite. This unique gift was presented to New York City in 1881 by the khedive of Egypt. Beyond the obelisk lies the **Great Lawn**, a pleasant spot to picnic or rest.

Across the way on the right is the **Metropolitan Museum of Art.** Its collection of more than three million works of art makes this the largest art museum in the Western Hemisphere. The museum is open Tuesday through Sunday but is closed on most holidays. Bicycle parking is available in the underground garage.

In many ways Central Park itself is a fine work of art. Although it has the appearance of a natural landscape, every square inch was meticulously planned and created by Frederick Law Olmsted and Calvert Vaux in the mid-nineteenth century. Before construction began in 1858, the area was a swampy dumping ground described by the *New York Post* as a "waste land, ugly and repulsive." Sixteen years and $14 million later, Olmsted and Vaux had created an 840-acre park that is enjoyed by more than three million people annually.

East Drive veers to the right as it passes the **Reservoir.** Actually, this body of water no longer serves as a functional reservoir since the city gets most of its drinking water from a series of large reservoirs upstate. If you wish, you may walk your bike along the jogging path and bridle path surrounding the reservoir (but please refrain from riding on these trails).

Continue beyond the waters of the Harlem Meer to begin the journey back south. Up to this point the park road has been either flat or downhill, but now it is time to pay the piper. As you loop past the 105th Street exit, you begin the climb up the park's aptly named "Great Hill." Thankfully, the ascent does not last terribly long before the road begins to descend once again.

Opposite the park's West 72nd Street entrance is **Strawberry Fields.** More than 160 species of trees, shrubs, and flowers from 150 countries follow the curved footpaths as they ascend a small hill. Named for the well-known song by the Beatles, Strawberry Fields is a living monument to the late John Lennon, who lived at 72nd Street and Central Park West.

The ride concludes in 5 blocks back at the West 67th Street park entrance. Care to take another lap?

For Further Information

Central Park General Information (212) 360–3456
Tavern on the Green (212) 873–3200
Wollman Memorial Rink (212) 517–4800
The Dairy (212) 397–3156
Central Park Carousel (212) 879–0244
Loeb Boathouse (212) 288–7281
Metropolitan Museum of Art (212) 535–7710

Manhattan
Upper Upper West Side

Mileage:	14
Terrain:	Rolling
Traffic:	Moderate to heavy
Facilities:	Rest rooms and water fountains throughout Riverside Park; rest room facilities and food vendors at Grant's Tomb, The Cloisters, and Tom's Restaurant
Things to see:	Riverside Park, Boat Basin, Promenade, Soldiers' and Sailors' Monument, Joan of Arc Memorial, Firemen's Memorial, Riverside Church, Grant's Tomb, Riverbank State Park, George Washington Bridge, Fort Tryon Park, The Cloisters, Columbia University, Morningside Park, Cathedral of St. John the Divine, Tom's Restaurant

Manhattan's furthest reaches often go ignored by tourists and visitors, who instead stay to the south of an artificial boundary, Central Park. And while some of the areas north of the park do not offer the best cycling conditions, this trip along the Hudson River takes cyclists through portions of Riverside Park and some of Manhattan's most attractive neighborhoods, stopping along the way at some of the city's most interesting landmarks. And you'll finally learn first-hand who is buried in Grant's Tomb.

Begin your journey at the corner of West 72nd Street and Riverside Drive. Here, you have a choice, either to head north on Riverside

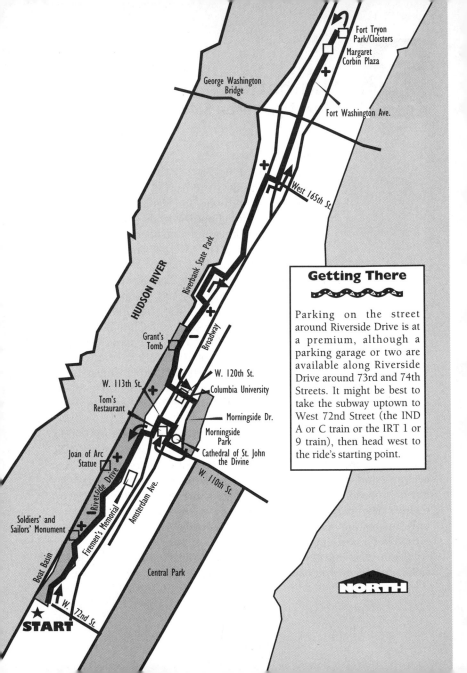

Fort Tryon Park/Cloisters

Margaret Corbin Plaza

George Washington Bridge

Fort Washington Ave.

West 165th St.

HUDSON RIVER

Riverbank State Park

Grant's Tomb

Broadway

W. 120th St.

Columbia University

W. 113th St.

Tom's Restaurant

Morningside Dr.

Morningside Park

Cathedral of St. John the Divine

Joan of Arc Statue

Riverside Drive

Amsterdam Ave.

W. 110th St.

Soldiers' and Sailors' Monument

Firemen's Memorial

Central Park

Boat Basin

W. 72nd St.

★ START

Getting There

Parking on the street around Riverside Drive is at a premium, although a parking garage or two are available along Riverside Drive around 73rd and 74th Streets. It might be best to take the subway uptown to West 72nd Street (the IND A or C train or the IRT 1 or 9 train), then head west to the ride's starting point.

NORTH

DIREC-TIONS at a glance

0.0	Start at 72nd Street and Riverside Drive; head north on Riverside Drive (or follow path through park).
1.0	Follow Riverside Drive to left at West 91st Street.
1.3	Veer left at West 97th Street to stay on Riverside Drive.

2.9 After Grant's Tomb, follow Riverside Drive across West 125th Street Viaduct.

3.5 Turn left at West 139th Street, onto pedestrian walkway into Riverbank Park. Continue through park to north exit road.

3.8 Turn left back onto Riverside Drive (now at West 145th Street).

4.9 Turn right onto West 165th Street.

5.0 Turn left onto Fort Washington Avenue.

6.4 At Margaret Corbin Plaza, head into Fort Tryon Park; afterwards, exit the park as you entered.

7.8 Turn right onto West 165th Street.

7.9 Turn left onto Riverside Drive.

10.3 Turn left at 120th Street/Columbia University.

10.6 Turn right onto Morningside Drive.

11.2 Turn right onto West 110th Street (Cathedral Parkway).

11.4 Turn right onto Amsterdam Avenue.

11.6 Turn left onto West 113th Street.

11.7 Turn left onto Broadway.

11.9 Turn right onto West 110th Street.

12.0 Turn right, then left onto Riverside Drive South.

14.0 Back at 72nd Street.

Drive (as the map shows) or to cut a swath through **Riverside Park**, which runs along the road's western side. Riverside Park was designed by Frederick Law Olmsted, renowned as co-architect of Manhattan's Central Park (Ride #2) and Brooklyn's Prospect Park (Ride #5). Construction of the park and the drive of the same name took place between 1875 and 1941, when the **Promenade** was finally completed. The choice either to follow the route through the park or on Riverside Drive is yours, although for purposes of measuring distances, we took the roadway. And don't worry, if you take one, but decide that you'd prefer switching to the other, there are plenty of opportunities along the way to move back and forth. Just one caveat up front: At several intersections, you will also find entranceways onto Henry Hudson Parkway. *Don't veer onto the parkway by mistake!*

If you are following the paths through the park, you'll shortly come to the **Boat Basin**; if you are following Riverside Drive, turn left at West 79th Street and continue to the traffic circle. The Boat Basin is one of the few spots in Manhattan where you can walk (or ride) right along the water's edge. Along with the smell of salt air, you'll find an armada of houseboats that a select group of Manhattanites call home. From the circle, follow the Promenade northward. At its end, if you're in season, you'll find a beautiful flower garden, which is cared for by local residents. You'll also see, to the right, the white marble columns of the **Soldiers' and Sailors' Monument**, dedicated to those who served in the Civil War.

Make your way back to Riverside Drive, either by retracing your path along the Promenade or by blazing a trail through the park, where you may rejoin the roadway at West 90th Street. Just ahead, at the fork in the road, lies the **Joan of Arc Memorial**, created in 1915 by the famous American sculptor Anna Vaughn Hyatt Huntington. The statue was commissioned three years earlier, in honor of the 500th anniversary of Joan of Arc's birth. Often called the Maid of Orléans, Joan of Arc remains a national heroine and patron saint of France who united the nation at a critical hour and decisively turned the Hundred Years' War in France's favor. Interestingly, the statue's pedestal contains fragments of France's Rheims Cathedral, where Joan of Arc played a pivotal role in uniting the French behind King Charles III, and stones from the Tower of Rouen, where she was burned at the stake in the town square two years after being branded as a heretic and rebel by both church and state. (Twenty five years later, the church retried her and pronounced her innocent.)

Continue on Riverside Drive northward, veering to the left as the road does at both West 91st and West 97th Streets. The **Firemen's Memorial**, at West 100th Street, is a huge monument erected in 1913 to commemorate the heroism of firefighters who do battle in "a war that never ends." The monument's bronze panel depicts three speeding horses pulling an old-fashioned fire wagon, racing toward a fire. Marble figures set to either side of the monument show a widow with her dead husband and another widow with her children, all poignantly displaying how firefighters risk their lives for society everyday.

Built in 1930, **Riverside Church** stands tall amidst the tree-lined surroundings near West 122nd Street. Though affiliated with the American Baptist Church and the United Church of Christ, Riverside Church offers interdenominational services. The Gothic edifice, adorned with statues reminiscent of the French cathedral at Chartres, will immediately draw your attention. The two striking stained-glass windows in the church's narthex, which depict the life of Christ, originally belonged to the 16th-century Cathedral of Bruges in Belgium. On Sunday afternoons, visitors can board elevators for a ride up twenty of the tower's twenty-two stories to the observation deck. By climbing two more stories to the top, you will pass by the tower's seventy-four-bell carillon—the largest in the world. From that height, the view of the Hudson River, Riverside Park, and New Jersey is breathtaking. The church is open daily; a modest admission fee is charged for the elevator ride up the bell tower.

Get back on the bike, but not for long, as **Grant's Tomb** (officially, the General Grant National Memorial) is just ahead on the left. And just *who* is buried there? Ulysses Simpson Grant, commander of the Union Army during much of the Civil War and subsequently elected President of the United States from 1869 to 1877, died in 1885 and was interred here after the monument was completed in 1897. His wife, Julia Dent Grant, was buried next to her husband after her death in 1902. The inscription above the door into the mausoleum reads "Let us have peace," from Grant's address to the Republican Party in 1868, when he accepted the nomination to run for the presidency. Busts of other Union generals and photographs illustrating Grant's life are found inside, as is a dome suspended above the sunken crypts of the President and First Lady. Grant's Tomb is open year-round but is closed on major holidays.

After Grant's Tomb, Riverside Park ends, but the ride continues to follow Riverside Drive across the 125th Street Viaduct. Once on the other side, the park picks up again, though is now noticeably narrower. At West 139th Street, turn left into the entrance to **Riverbank State Park**. Built atop a sewage treatment plant, Riverbank Park is a popular attraction for residents of Morningside Heights and West Harlem. Within its twenty-eight acres are two swimming pools, tennis courts, a track, and a rink that is set up for ice-skating in the winter and roller- and inline-skating during spring, summer, and autumn. In addition, the park's several playgrounds and walking paths all offer splendid views of the Hudson River, George Washington Bridge, and New Jersey Palisades.

Exit the state park through its north gate at West 145th Street, turn left, and continue north on Riverside Drive. One mile later, turn right onto West 165th Street, then quickly left onto Fort Washington Avenue, passing Columbia Presbyterian Hospital. When you cross under the access road to the **George Washington Bridge** at West 179th Street, look for the small signs that direct cyclists to the bridge's bikeway for a trip into New Jersey. Though we don't detail the route here, the bikeway is a great adventure for those who wish to divert for a short (or long) side trip into the Garden State.

A final climb brings you to Margaret Corbin Plaza and **Fort Tryon Park**. Encompassing sixty-two acres, bucolic Fort Tryon Park is the antithesis of lower Manhattan. Here, in place of the hustle and bustle of the big city, are rolling hills, manicured terraces, and beautiful gardens. Bird songs, not blaring horns, greet your ears. Fort Tryon is named for William Tryon, the last English civilian governor of New York before the American Revolution. Thanks to its commanding view of the Hudson, Fort Tryon played a pivotal role in the war, though it ultimately fell to British control in November 1776.

Follow Park Drive into the park, passing Fort Tryon on the left, and veering to the right up ahead to circle **The Cloisters**. The Cloisters, administered by the Metropolitan Museum of Art, appears the quintessential medieval monastery. Many hours can easily be spent wandering from hall to hall, admiring countless sculptures, stained-glass windows, gardens, and other fine examples of medieval art. While Fort Tryon Park is open daily, the Cloisters is open Tuesdays through Sundays throughout the year. An $8.00 admission is charged for the museum, but the park is free.

Leave Fort Tryon Park as you entered it and head south on Fort Washington Avenue. Continue to West 165th Street, where the route turns right, then left 1 block later to return to Riverside Drive. Turn left onto West 120th Street for an impromptu trip through **Columbia University**. Although the "official route" continues straight on West 120th Street, we encourage you to veer off temporarily to explore the campus.

Continue east to Morningside Drive, then turn right. Bordering the road to the left is **Morningside Park**. Follow the road downhill, turn right at the bottom onto West 110th Street (also known here as Cathedral Parkway), then right again onto Amsterdam Avenue. Spanning the block between Morningside Drive and Amsterdam Avenue is the **Cathedral of St. John the Divine**, the largest Episcopal cathedral in New York City, and one of the largest in the world. Think of this edifice, as a work in progress. Construction began in 1892, though delays and redesigns continue to hamper completion even to this day. While much of the cathedral is complete, it is estimated that another century may be needed to finish the towers, sacristy, and carvings. Delays are understandable when one considers the magnitude of the project. One look at the double set of bronze entryway doors gives a good indication, as each weighs three tons. Observant visitors will see that the left-hand set of doors bears a scene from the Old Testament, while the right-hand pair depicts a New Testament scene. Inside, the magnificent rose window is constructed of an estimated 10,000 pieces of glass. Majestic columns of granite surround the sanctuary and high altar. The Cathedral is open daily throughout the year, with one-hour guided tours given once a day every day except Mondays; call ahead for exact times.

Continue on Amsterdam Avenue to West 113th Street, then turn left. One block ahead, turn left onto Broadway. One block south on Broadway, on the northeast corner of West 112th Street (on your left), is a facade that should be familiar to nearly everyone who has watched television in the 1990s: **Tom's Restaurant**. For nine years, Tom's was used as exterior shots for the restaurant scenes in the popular television show *Seinfeld*. It was here that Jerry, Elaine, George, and Kramer frequently met to talk about nothing. Though the interior doesn't match that shown on TV, you still might want to stop in and grab a bite.

Continue to West 110th Street, then turn right to zigzag back onto Riverside Drive South. Continue on this final leg of the trip back to the ride's starting point at West 72nd Street.

For Further Information

Boat Basin (212) 496–2105
Cathedral of St. John the Divine (212) 316–7540
The Cloisters (212) 923–3700
Columbia University (212) 854–4900
Grant's Tomb (212) 666–1640
Riverbank State Park (212) 694–3600
Riverside Church (212) 870–6700
Riverside Park (212) 408–0264
Tom's Restaurant (212) 864–6137

Manhattan/Brooklyn
A Two-Borough Tour

Mileage:	8
Terrain:	Flat
Traffic:	Moderate to heavy
Facilities:	Rest rooms, water fountains, and food stops in and around South Street Seaport
Things to see:	South Street Seaport, St. Paul's Chapel, Brooklyn Bridge, Brooklyn Heights, Brooklyn Historical Society

Step back in time to the Manhattan of the nineteenth century. Far down on the Lower East Side, life centers around the city's seaport, the heart of worldwide trade and commerce. Here, ships heavily laden with all sorts of cargo regularly sail in and out of port, bound for all corners of the globe.

Across the East River, Brooklyn is a completely different world. Tree-lined cobblestoned streets flanked by residences create a sense of tranquility, in sharp contrast to the hectic pace of the big city.

This ride offers a tour of these two diverse neighborhoods. Start at the famed **South Street Seaport**, near the corner of South and Fulton Streets. One hundred years ago, all goods shipped into and out of New York passed through the seaport. Abandoned shortly after the turn of the century when shipping moved to piers in the Hudson River, the seaport was resurrected in the 1960s as historic preservation efforts got underway.

Between South and Water Streets, Fulton Street was converted into a pedestrian mall lined with shops and restaurants. Just up Fulton on the right is the Fulton Market Building, the fourth market to be built on this site since 1822. It houses food and souvenir outlets.

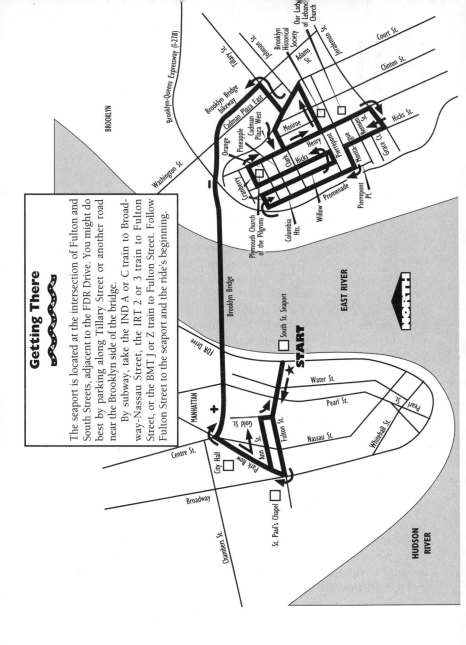

Getting There

The seaport is located at the intersection of Fulton and South Streets, adjacent to the FDR Drive. You might do best by parking along Tillary Street or another road near the Brooklyn side of the bridge.

By subway, take the IND A or C train to Broadway-Nassau Street, the IRT 2 or 3 train to Fulton Street, or the BMT J or Z train to Fulton Street. Follow Fulton Street to the seaport and the ride's beginning.

BROOKLYN

Brooklyn-Queens Expressway (I-278)

Our Lady of Lebanon Church

Court St.

Brooklyn Historical Society

Johnson St.

Adams St.

Clinton St.

Tillary St.

Joralemon St.

Brooklyn Bridge bikeway

Hicks St.

Cadman Plaza East

Cadman Plaza West

Monroe

Ransen St.

Grace Ct.

Pierrepont

Montague

Orange

Pineapple

Henry

Hicks

Clark

Cranberry

Promenade

Pierrepont Pl.

Willow

Plymouth Church of the Pilgrims

Columbia Hts.

Washington St.

EAST RIVER

NORTH

Brooklyn Bridge

FDR Drive

South St. Seaport

START

Water St.

Pearl St.

Pearl St.

MANHATTAN

Gold St.

Ann St.

Fulton St.

Nassau St.

Whitehall St.

Centre St.

City Hall

Park Row

Broadway

St. Paul's Chapel

Chambers St.

HUDSON RIVER

DIREC- TIONS at a glance

0.0	Head west on Fulton Street from South Street.
0.5	Right onto Broadway.
0.6	Right onto Park Row.
0.7	Left onto Centre Street.
0.8	Follow signs toward Brooklyn Bridge bicycle/pedestrian path.
2.2	Leaving bridge, turn right onto Tillary Street.
2.3	Right onto Cadman Plaza West.
2.4	Left onto Clark Street.
2.5	Left onto Henry Street.
2.8	Right onto Joralemon Street.
2.9	Right onto Hicks Street.
3.1	Left onto Montague Street.
3.2	Right onto Pierrepont Place.
3.3	Left onto Columbia Heights.
3.6	Right onto Cranberry Street.
3.7	Right onto Willow Street.
4.0	Left onto Pierrepont Street.
4.1	Left onto Hicks Street.
4.4	Right onto Cranberry Street.
4.5	Right onto Henry Street.
4.8	Left onto Pierrepont Street.
5.0	Left onto Cadman Plaza West.
5.1	Right onto Tillary Street.
5.2	Left onto Brooklyn Bridge bikeway.
6.6	Left onto Park Row.
6.9	Left onto Ann Street.
7.1	Right onto Gold Street.
7.2	Left onto Fulton Street.
7.5	Back at Fulton and South Streets.

Do you smell fish? Probably, since the South Street side of the building is home to the Fulton Fish Market. The fish is fresh daily; the market has been operating pierside for more than 200 years.

Across from the market, under the elevated FDR Drive, is the Pier 17 Pavilion. Inside you will find more than a hundred shops and restaurants. The view from the promenade is spectacular; upriver lie the Brooklyn and Manhattan Bridges; across the East River is Brooklyn Heights (your ultimate destination); downriver is the New York Harbor. You also have a great view of the historic ships moored at Piers 15 and 16. The tall ships are perhaps the most recognizable feature of the seaport. The grandest vessel there is the *Peking* (built in 1911), the second largest sailing ship in existence. All are worth a visit.

Return to the Fulton Street mall and continue down to Water Street. One block north, at Front and Beekman Streets, you will find the Seaport's visitors' center, open daily except Thanksgiving, Christmas, and New Year's Day. There you can learn of the many other attractions that await visitors to this fascinating part of New York City.

But now it is time for us to cast off. Pedal westward on Fulton to the intersection with Broadway, then make a right. (Note that since your route flows against the traffic on Broadway, you must dismount your bike and walk for 1 block.)

Across Broadway is **St. Paul's Chapel**, the oldest church in Manhattan. You can't miss it; the churchyard takes up the entire block. Most of the chapel was completed in 1766, though the spire and portico facing Broadway were constructed in 1794.

Take the next right onto Park Row and get back on your bike. Skirting the edge of City Hall Park, wind along Park Row as it heads toward the **Brooklyn Bridge**. As your route joins Centre Street, follow the signs as they lead toward the bridge's central bicycle/pedestrian path. Though the path begins with a climb, the outstanding view of lower Manhattan makes it worth the effort!

Brooklyn Bridge was the first of the city's great bridges. In 1869 John Roebling was commissioned to design the bridge, which had been branded "impossible." Though Roebling died before the bridge was finished, his son, Washington, directed the effort to its successful completion. When it opened in 1883, the Brooklyn Bridge was hailed as the "eighth wonder of the world" and it remains today as a monument to American creativity and genius.

Follow the bike-path signs as you descend the Brooklyn side of the bridge and take a right onto Tillary Street. Stay on the "diamond" bike lane as it winds westward. Turn right onto Cadman Plaza West, then left onto Clark Street to enter **Brooklyn Heights**. Home to the twin cousins Patty and Cathy Lane of the classic TV sitcom *The Patty Duke Show*, Brooklyn Heights has retained much of its charm from a century ago, when it was Manhattan's first suburb.

After 2 short blocks, turn left onto Henry Street. A narrow lane shaded by trees and lined with shoulder-to-shoulder homes, Henry typifies the streets of Brooklyn Heights. Continue to the intersection with Remsen Street, then sidestep for a quick visit to Our Lady of Lebanon Church. Adding to the uniqueness of its Romanesque Revival–style architecture are the church doors, salvaged from the shipwrecked ocean liner *Normandie*.

Back on Henry, watch for Hunts Lane, a small dead-end street on the left. Hunts Lane is a marvelous mews lined with a number of restored carriage houses that were once stables for the affluent residents of nearby Remsen Street.

Turn right twice, once onto Joralemon Street, then again, in 1 block, onto Hicks Street. There, you will pass Grace Church on the left and Grace Court Alley across the way. Like Hunts Lane, Grace Court Alley originally contained stables and carriage houses owned by wealthy local residents.

At Montague Street turn left and continue all the way to its end. You now have a choice to make. You may continue straight onto the Brooklyn Heights Promenade, but bear in mind that bicycle riding is prohibited for its entire length. You wouldn't want to rush here, anyway. Take the time to enjoy the breathtaking view of the Manhattan skyline and lower New York Harbor. Trees, flowers, and benches line the promenade, making it a wonderful place for a midride break.

If you prefer to stay on your bike instead, turn right onto Pierrepont Place. At its end, swerve left to continue on Columbia Heights. These two streets feature some of the finest brownstone homes in all of New York City.

Wind to the right onto Cranberry Street, then right again onto Willow Street. Some widely varied architecture adds to the delight of these residential roads. Especially noteworthy is the row of homes from 151 to 159 Willow Street. Though you would never guess it, a tunnel used to connect 159 and 151, the latter once being a stable.

A pair of quick lefts will take you from Willow to Pierrepont Street and finally onto Hicks Street, heading north again. You may feel as if you're traveling through a fruit salad, as you pass streets with names like Pineapple and Orange. Just down Orange on the right is the Plymouth Church of the Pilgrims. The church played a key role in the Underground Railroad, which was used to smuggle slaves to freedom before the Civil War.

Stay on Hicks for 1 more block to Cranberry Street, where the route makes another right. A second right puts you back on Henry Street. Continue on Henry for 5 blocks, then turn left onto Pierrepont Street. Before leaving Brooklyn Heights stop at the **Brooklyn Historical Society's** home at the corner of Pierrepont and Clinton Streets. Its collection of Brooklyn memorabilia ranges from playing equipment used by the Brooklyn Dodgers to a huge cast-iron eagle, once the symbol of the now-defunct *Brooklyn Eagle* newspaper. The society is open Tuesdays through Sundays and there is a nominal admission charge.

Turn left onto Cadman Plaza West, then right onto Tillary Street to join the Brooklyn Bridge bikeway. At the end of the bikeway, turn left at Centre Street and proceed onto Park Row. Just before Broadway take a left onto Ann Street. A right in a couple of blocks onto Gold Street and a left onto Fulton Street will bring you back to the seaport. (If you wish, continue south on Broadway toward Battery Park and follow Ride #1 for an excursion into Greenwich Village.)

For Further Information

South Street Seaport (212) 669–9424
Brooklyn Historical Society (718) 624–0890

Brooklyn
Brooklyn Greenway

Mileage:	22 or 35
Terrain:	Flat
Traffic:	Light in park and on bikeways, heavy elsewhere
Facilities:	Rest rooms and water fountains within Prospect Park as well as at the New York Aquarium
Things to see:	Prospect Park, Grand Army Plaza, Brooklyn Botanic Garden, Brooklyn Public Library, Brooklyn Museum, Coney Island, New York Aquarium, Verrazano-Narrows Bridge

Even as you read this, ambitious plans are underfoot to create a "greenway" of hiking and biking trails that will extend for 40 miles, from the Atlantic Ocean at Coney Island in Brooklyn to the beginning of Long Island Sound at Fort Totten in Queens. Along the way the route will connect thirteen parks, two botanic gardens, three lakes, and many other cultural, historic, and recreational centers. This is the dream of the Neighborhood Open Space Coalition, a nonprofit group whose aim is to preserve and improve the city's outdoors. On this ride you will get a chance to preview some of the areas that will form the Brooklyn portion of the Greenway, while Ride #7 details much of the Queens end of the Greenway.

Actually, this is two rides in one. Both originate from Park Circle, adjacent to the south entrance of **Prospect Park.** The first stage is a quick loop of the park itself. Proceed through the entrance and join the marked bike route as it travels counterclockwise along Park Drive.

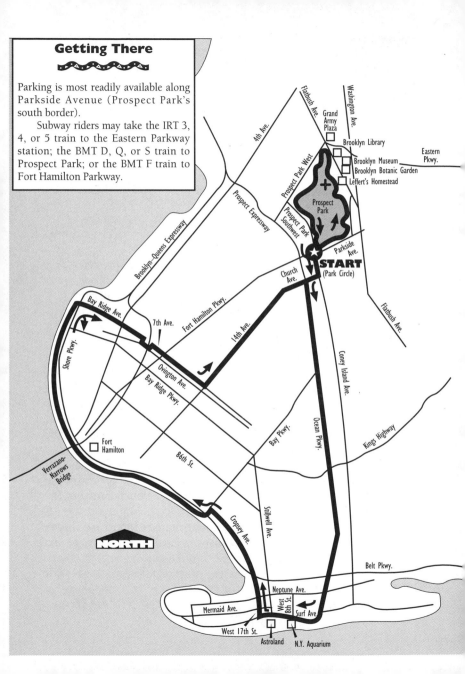

Getting There

Parking is most readily available along Parkside Avenue (Prospect Park's south border).

Subway riders may take the IRT 3, 4, or 5 train to the Eastern Parkway station; the BMT D, Q, or S train to Prospect Park; or the BMT F train to Fort Hamilton Parkway.

Flatbush Ave.

Washington Ave.

Grand Army Plaza

Brooklyn Library

4th Ave.

Prospect Park West

Brooklyn Museum

Eastern Pkwy.

Brooklyn Botanic Garden

Leffert's Homestead

Prospect Expressway

Prospect Park

Prospect Park Southwest

Parkside Ave.

START
(Park Circle)

Brooklyn-Queens Expressway

Church Ave.

Flatbush Ave.

Bay Ridge Ave.

Fort Hamilton Pkwy.

7th Ave.

14th Ave.

Coney Island Ave.

Shore Pkwy.

Ovington Ave.

Bay Ridge Pkwy.

Fort Hamilton

86th St.

Bay Pkwy.

Ocean Pkwy.

Kings Highway

Verrazano-Narrows Bridge

Cropsey Ave.

Stillwell Ave.

NORTH

Belt Pkwy.

Neptune Ave.

West 8th St.

Mermaid Ave.

Surf Ave.

West 17th St.

Astroland

N.Y. Aquarium

**DIREC-
TIONS
at a glance**

0.0	Begin at Park Circle. Enter park.	
1.8	Top of park at Grand Army Plaza.	
3.7	Exit park toward Park Circle. Travel counterclockwise around circle.	
3.8	Right onto Coney Island Avenue.	
4.1	Right onto Church Avenue.	
4.3	Left onto Ocean Parkway bikeway.	
9.1	Follow road to right onto Surf Avenue.	
10.1	Right onto West 17th Street.	
10.3	Cross Neptune Avenue and join Cropsey Avenue.	
11.8	Left onto Bay Parkway.	
12.0	Cross under Shore (Belt) Parkway and join bikeway on right.	
16.7	Bikeway ends at pier opposite Bay Ridge Avenue. To return, either turn around or continue on Bay Ridge Avenue.	
17.8	Right onto BQE service road.	
17.9	Left onto Ovington Avenue.	
18.0	Left onto 7th Avenue.	
18.1	Right onto Bay Ridge Avenue.	
18.9	Left onto 14th Avenue.	
20.7	Veer right to continue on Church Avenue.	
21.3	Left onto Coney Island Avenue.	
21.6	Back at Park Circle.	

The first thing you are bound to notice inside the park is Prospect Lake, a tranquil body of water surrounded by open meadow. The lake's boathouse, where visitors once rented boats for quiet afternoon cruises, acts as the park's visitors' center.

A little farther along Park Drive, off to the right, is Leffert's Homestead, a restored Dutch colonial farmhouse built in 1783. A museum inside features colonial furniture along with a variety of changing exhibits. The homestead is open weekends year-round, as well as Wednesday through Friday from April through December.

A little ways past the right-hand turn toward Leffert's Homestead, get ready to pedal up the park's biggest climb. The hill tops out just before the park's north gate. Outside the gate, at the intersection of Flatbush Avenue and Eastern Parkway, is **Grand Army Plaza**. At the head of the plaza stands the majestic Triumphal Arch, which commemorates the Union's victory in the Civil War. Atop the arch is the sculpture of a mighty horse-drawn chariot, while statues of the army and navy adorn either side.

Across Flatbush Avenue from the plaza is the **Brooklyn Botanic Garden**. The grounds feature thousands of different species of flowers, trees, and bushes set in half a dozen theme gardens. Of special interest is the Steinhardt Conservatory, a magnificent complex of greenhouses simulating many contrasting environments. Admission to the garden is free, though there is a small charge to visit the conservatory.

Set at the southeastern corner of Eastern Parkway and Flatbush Avenue is the **Brooklyn Public Library**. Inside, more than 1.5 million volumes await bibliophiles. Next door to the library, the **Brooklyn Museum** features an amazingly wide selection of exhibits throughout its five floors. These range from totem poles and masks to a granite sarcophagus dating to 2500 B.C. Be sure to stop at both of these fascinating places and allow enough time for your visit.

Return to Prospect Park, continuing counterclockwise along the marked bike lane. Happily, this part of the path is downhill! Stay on the lane toward the south gate, where you will see signs leading toward Ocean Parkway and the ride's second stage to Coney Island—and, ultimately, into Bay Ridge.

Ocean Parkway was the world's second parkway when it opened in 1874. On June 15, 1895, the first-ever bikeway was opened to the cycling public. It ran along Ocean Parkway for 5 miles, from Prospect Park to Coney Island. On that inaugural day the League of American Wheelmen sponsored a ride that attracted more than 10,000 participants!

Due to construction along both Prospect Expressway and Ocean Parkway in 1974, the bikeway north of Church Avenue was almost completely eliminated. Getting from the park to the parkway is now a bit more complicated and a bit more hazardous. Here's how to do it:

Carefully circle three-quarters of the way around Park Circle to Coney Island Avenue; then turn right. Stay on Coney Island Avenue until you come to Church Avenue; take another right.

Once at the intersection of Church Avenue and Ocean Parkway, proceed southward on the bikeway, adjacent to the latter's southbound traffic lane. Trees overhang the route, offering cooling shade on what can be a hot route. A black metal divider runs the entire length of the bikeway in an attempt to keep pedestrians out of the cyclists' way and vice versa. Please observe the rule that restricts bike riding to one-half of the path only (the half closer to the parkway).

Bear right at the end of the bikeway onto Surf Avenue. Welcome to **Coney Island**. The name immediately conjures up images of thundering roller coasters, giant Ferris wheels, and hot dogs galore, but when the Dutch first landed here in the early 1600s, all they found were rabbits. The island was full of them. In fact, the name *Coney Island* is an Americanized version of the original Dutch name, *Konijn Eiland,* meaning "rabbit island."

By the 1830s the rabbits had been replaced by elegant hotels, lavish casinos, and throngs of wealthy beach goers. The 1880s saw Coney Island change dramatically as the resort turned into a huge amusement park.

Though the area fell on hard times beginning in the 1950s, a few of the original rides remain open at Astroland. And you can still get a hot dog from the first "Nathan's Famous" hot dog stand, though it will cost more than the nickel Nathan Handwerker used to charge.

The **New York Aquarium** relocated to Coney Island from Manhattan's Battery Park in 1957. Located on the corner of Surf Avenue and West 8th Street, the aquarium features both indoor and outdoor exhibits. Inside, you can see more than 300 species of fishes, while outside, large tanks hold whales, dolphins, sea lions, and penguins. The aquarium is open daily, with a modest admission charge.

Though the Greenway ends here, our route continues. Across from the rusting remains of the Coney Island Parachute Jump, turn right onto West 17th Street and cross Coney Island Inlet to join Cropsey Avenue. Stay on Cropsey for 1.5 miles to the intersection with Bay Parkway. Turn left and go under Shore Parkway (a.k.a. Belt

Parkway). When you emerge on the other side, you will find yourself in a huge parking lot. Ahead are two large buildings; one houses a Toys-R-Us store. As you enter the lot, look to the right for a small sign leading to Shore Bikeway.

The bikeway closely follows the curved shoreline of Brooklyn. Across the water you can see South Beach on Staten Island, while looming up ahead is the **Verrazano-Narrows Bridge.** Opened in November 1964, the Verrazano spans 13,700 feet, the longest span of any suspension bridge.

Dwarfed by the Verrazano is Fort Wadsworth, which teamed with Fort Hamilton in Brooklyn to defend the port of New York against invasion during colonial times.

The bikeway ends at a concrete pier that juts out into the harbor. From here you have a dramatic view of lower Manhattan, Staten Island, the Statue of Liberty, Ellis Island, and the Verrazano.

To return to Prospect Park, you may either reverse the route or cut across Brooklyn on any of a number of different roads (the map offers one possibility). If you choose the latter, please keep in mind that much of the road surface in this area is rutted and potentially damaging to delicate road bicycles. Mountain bikers, on the other hand, may find the terrain invigorating. All riders should be especially watchful of traffic.

For Further Information

Prospect Park (718) 788–0055
Brooklyn Botanic Garden (718) 622–4433
Brooklyn Public Library (718) 780–7700
New York Aquarium (718) 266–8711
Neighborhood Open Space Coalition (212) 513–7555

Queens/Brooklyn
Jamaica Bay Roundabout

Mileage:	20
Terrain:	Flat
Traffic:	Light (nonexistent on bikeways)
Facilities:	Rest rooms, food stops, and water fountains at the Jamaica Bay Wildlife Area, Jacob Riis Park, Floyd Bennett Field, and Canarsie Pier; several fast-food and local restaurants along Beach Channel Drive; food also available at Carnarsie Pier
Things to see:	Gateway National Recreation Area, Jamaica Bay Wildlife Refuge, Rockaway Boardwalk, Jacob Riis Park, Fort Tilden Park, Floyd Bennett Field, Canarsie Pier

When it opened on October 27, 1972, **Gateway National Recreation Area** integrated several local and county parks in a necklace of unique outdoor facilities that string together like pearls around New York Harbor. Included in this, the country's largest national recreation area, are Sandy Hook in New Jersey; Great Kills (visited in Ride #11), Miller Field, and Fort Wadsworth on Staten Island; and the Jamaica Bay area in Queens and Brooklyn, the focus of this ride.

The Jamaica Bay portion of the Gateway National Recreation Area, comprises the Jamaica Bay Wildlife Refuge, Jacob Riis Park, Fort Tilden Park, Breezy Point Park, and Floyd Bennett Field. All can be visited by bicycle by riding along some of the most scenic roadways in New York City.

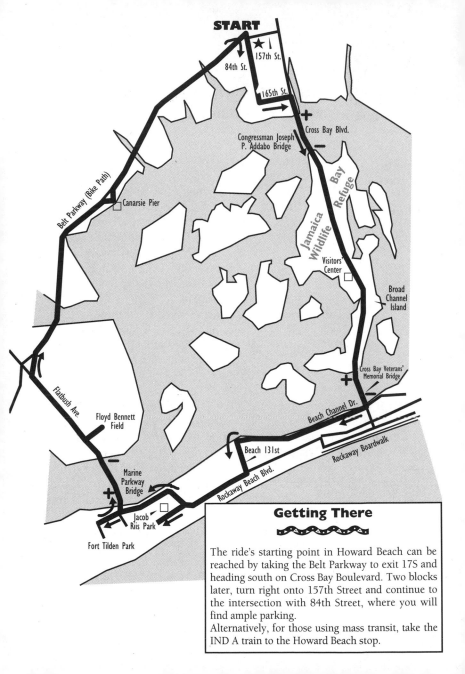

START

157th St.

84th St.

165th St.

Cross Bay Blvd.

Congressman Joseph
P. Addabo Bridge

Belt Parkway (Bike Path)

Canarsie Pier

Bay Refuge

Jamaica Wildlife

Visitors'
Center

Broad
Channel
Island

Cross Bay Veterans'
Memorial Bridge

Flatbush Ave.

Floyd Bennett
Field

Beach Channel Dr.

Beach 131st

Rockaway Boardwalk

Rockaway Beach Blvd.

Marine
Parkway
Bridge

Jacob
Riis Park

Fort Tilden Park

Getting There

The ride's starting point in Howard Beach can be reached by taking the Belt Parkway to exit 17S and heading south on Cross Bay Boulevard. Two blocks later, turn right onto 157th Street and continue to the intersection with 84th Street, where you will find ample parking.

Alternatively, for those using mass transit, take the IND A train to the Howard Beach stop.

DIREC-TIONS at a glance

0.0 From St. Helen's Church at the corner of 84th Street and 157th Avenue, head south on 84th Street.

0.9 At T intersection, turn left onto 165th Avenue.

1.4 Turn right onto Cross Bay Boulevard, then up over Congressman Joseph P. Addabo Bridge. After bridge, follow bike lane (white diamonds).

3.7 Turn left into Gateway National Recreation Area Wildlife Refuge exhibit area.

5.3 At toll gate, cross road and proceed over Cross Bay Veteran's Memorial Bridge using the sidewalk on the east (left) side of the bridge.

6.1 Come off bridge and turn left onto Beach Channel Drive.

8.1 Turn left onto Beach 131st Street (sign says B131 ST).

8.5 Turn right onto Rockaway Beach Boulevard. (A left turn down any of the side roads will lead to the beach.)

9.4 Enter Jacob Riis Park by following road halfway around traffic circle. Be careful as you cross the lanes of traffic!

9.8 After a visit to Riis Park, follow road to left after traffic circle, go up and over bridge and back onto Beach Channel Boulevard.

10.4 At fork with Marine Parkway Bridge, follow road to the right, toward "Breezy Point."

11.1 Turn left into Fort Tilden Park. Afterward, turn right out of exit to return to the Marine Parkway Bridge.

11.7 At Beach 169th Street, shift onto the sidewalk (along the left, or west, side of road) to cross Marine Parkway Bridge. After passing alongside the toll gate, cross Flatbush Avenue to rejoin traffic.

12.8 Turn right into Floyd Bennett Field. Be prepared to ride 4 or more miles throughout the park during your visit. When tour is done, exit through the park's main gate and turn right onto the Flatbush Avenue Bikeway.

14.0 Turn right to follow the Belt Parkway Bikeway toward the east.

16.9 Follow bikeway to the right, pausing at Canarsie Pier.

19.9 Turn right off bikeway onto 84th Street (unmarked at the bikeway intersection) toward St. Helen's Church (yellow brick).

20.0 Back at 84th Street and 157th Avenue and the ride's beginning.

The ride disembarks from the parking lot of St. Helen's Church in Howard Beach, Queens. The church, located on the corner of 84th Street and 157th Avenue (also known as Monsignor McGuinness Place), is highlighted by a distinctive facade of yellow brick. Head south on 84th Street through a pleasant neighborhood of one- and two-story homes. As you travel along, look to the right at each intersection, toward 83rd Street, to see the first signs of Jamaica Bay. If you want, take a short side diversion to view the scene close up, but return to 84th Street to continue; 83rd Street is one-way, the wrong way.

At the end of 84th Street, turn left onto 165th Street, which parallels marshland along the right side of the road. About a half mile ahead, turn right onto Cross Bay Boulevard and proceed across Congressman Joseph P. Addabo Bridge. The bicycle-advocacy organization Transportation Alternatives proclaims this the winner of its "Fiboro Award for Best Bridge" for its wide bike lane separated from the three lanes of vehicular traffic. The riding surface is smooth and the upward slope is slow enough to be pedaled by most cyclists without much trouble. A sidewalk also passes along the roadway, but is usually populated with folks fishing for "the big one." As such, cyclists are strongly urged to stay on the road.

Coasting down the bridge, the bike lane enters onto Broad Channel Island. The wide road expanse passes through a portion of

Jamaica Bay Wildlife Refuge. The refuge is famous as one of the finest birdwatching areas along the entire East Coast. Thousands of water, land, and shore birds stop here each year during the spring and autumn migration seasons. Several pull-offs are found along the road, though most people will want to continue south for about a mile or so to the area's visitors' center, on the right. Pull in, park, and chain your bike to one of the bike racks, and take a short side trip inside. You will find rest rooms, a water fountain, book shop, and an exhibit area. Visitors can also explore the refuge's unique ecological habitats along a wonderful 1.5-mile hiking trail around a manmade freshwater pond (sorry, no bikes allowed) by obtaining a free hiking permit in the visitors' center, open every day from 8:30 A.M. to 5:00 P.M.

From the visitors' center, turn right to continue south on Cross Bay Boulevard. Shortly, the population begins to grow as you enter the seaside village of Broad Channel. Looking more like some areas on Cape Cod than Queens, Broad Channel includes many small shops and even more boats. Be careful as you approach the area, as the bike lane veers into the road to allow cars to park next to the curb. Remain especially vigilant for that suddenly opening car door!

Leaving Broad Channel, continue to the Cross Bay Veteran's Memorial Bridge. Signs just before the toll gate direct cyclists and pedestrians to a narrow sidewalk along the east side of the bridge; cyclists are not allowed on the bridge's roadway. This is a popular place, especially on a warm summer day, so be careful of anyone walking or fishing as you pedal up and over the bridge.

As you coast off of the bridge, you exit onto Beach Channel Drive. Did somebody say McDonald's? If so, you'll be happy to find a pair of the golden arches waiting for you at the foot of the bridge. (Just to be fair, you'll also come to a Wendy's and a delicatessen in about a mile.) Veer left onto Beach Channel Drive to head west along the north shore of Rockaway Island. Shortly, pass Beach Channel High School on the right and, not long afterward, look for elevated tracks of the Rockaway subway line on the left. Continuing along, you will enjoy some nice views of the distant Manhattan skyline, with the Empire State Building and World Trade Center rising high above the rest. Later, as the road veers slightly to the left, watch for the Verrazano-Narrows Bridge in the distance and, closer, the Marine Bridge.

As you head west along Beach Channel Drive, notice how most of the side streets are one-way, with the odd-numbered streets taking traffic to the south and even-numbered streets heading north. If you wish, take any of the odd-numbered streets for a quick side trip to the Atlantic Ocean. Depending on where you turn south, you might also be able to visit the famous Rockaway Boardwalk. The boardwalk spans the beach to Beach 109th Street, where it terminates.

The ride itself turns left onto Beach 131st Street (labeled B131 ST on road signs) and travels through the pleasant residential area of Belle Harbor. Beautiful homes line the streets, painting a picture of serenity contrasted against the denser population and heavier traffic that stay to the east, closer to the bridge.

Turn right onto Rockaway Beach Boulevard and continue west. In just over a mile, the route enters Jacob Riis Park. Follow the road halfway around the traffic circle, being careful as you cross lanes of traffic! Riis Park, named for the famed photographer who chronicled the plight of the city's immigrant population in the early twentieth century, features several New York landmarks, including the famous bathhouse, boardwalk, and outdoor clock. Bathroom facilities and water fountains are available, although they are only operable during the summer.

Return to the traffic circle going three-quarters of the way around, then go up and over a small bridge to land back on Beach Channel Drive. Just ahead, at the fork, follow the sign to BREEZY POINT toward the right.

Turn left into Fort Tilden Park and tour this former military encampment. Encompassing 317 acres, this Army base was decommissioned in 1974 and is now part of the Gateway National Recreation Area. Although closed to bathing, you'll often find people fishing along the park's natural sand dunes, one of the last remaining dune systems in New York City, as well as cyclists touring the camp's many untraveled roads and hikers exploring the abandoned Army buildings. The Fort Tilden Visitors' Center is open daily from 8:30 A.M. to 5:00 P.M.

Leaving Fort Tilden, turn right back onto Beach Channel Drive and trace the route back to the Marine Parkway Bridge. To cross, you will have to ride along the sidewalk on the left, or west, side of the bridge since cyclists are not allowed on the roadway (good thing, since it has a metal grating surface). As before, be careful for anyone walking or fishing from along the bridge.

The bridge empties onto Flatbush Avenue. Welcome to Brooklyn! After passing alongside the toll gate (no toll for cyclists), carefully cross the street to rejoin traffic. Flatbush Avenue has several lanes for automotive traffic but only a narrow shoulder for cyclists, so proceed with caution.

About 1.5 miles after the bridge, turn right into Floyd Bennett Field, another part of the Gateway National Recreation Area. If you are pressed for time, there are rest rooms and a water fountain right at the park's entrance, but try to take the time to tour the park by bicycle, to relive some important moments in aviation history. You'll find miles and miles of traffic-free cycling as you pedal along the field's abandoned runways and access roads.

The airfield is named for pilot Floyd Bennett, who in 1926, along with Admiral Richard Byrd, was first to fly over the North Pole. Opened five years later, Bennett Field was New York City's first municipal airport, created long before either LaGuardia or Kennedy Airports. It was here that Wiley Post took off to set his round-the-world flying record in 1933, and Howard Hughes departed from here to break that record in 1938. Other famous pilots to originate flights from the field include Amelia Earhart, Jimmy Doolittle, Jacqueline Cochran, and Douglas Corrigan, who earned the nickname "Wrong-Way Corrigan" for mistakenly flying east to Ireland instead of west to California. At the beginning of World War II, the field was closed to commercial and private traffic and turned over to the military. In 1941, a Naval Air Station was constructed, which stayed in service through the Vietnam War. The airfield closed in 1972 and became part of the Gateway National Recreation Area.

Today, the field is again alive with activity as volunteers and park employees restore vintage aircraft, such as a C-47 transport, a World War II cargo aircraft; an H-3 Coast Guard helicopter; and an amphibious PBY Catalina, used during World War II for antisubmarine patrols. The Ryan Visitors' Center is open daily from 8:30 A.M. to 5:00 P.M.

Upon exiting Floyd Bennett Field, turn right onto the Flatbush Avenue Bikeway. The bikeway, paralleling the road, takes you past the front of the airfield, affording another view of any vintage aircraft that might be parked on display. One mile ahead, turn right onto the Belt Parkway Bikeway, where the route turns eastward. The Belt Bikeway features a smooth surface, at least for now, as it skirts along the Belt Parkway's eastbound lanes, heading back into Queens. Before they embark, cyclists should note that the Belt Bikeway presents certain challenges. For one, as it crosses several small bridges, the bikeway comes quite close to the parkway itself. The first two bridges do not have any physical guardrails between the bikeway and parkway, other than an elevated height, which might make some riders a bit nervous. The bikeway surface over the bridges is also quite rough and rutted, making cycling difficult. Our best advice is to get off your bike and walk across, then remount afterwards. A second problem is that, a few miles up ahead, the bikeway disappears for about a mile. But more on that later.

Follow the bikeway toward Canarsie Pier. Built in the 1920s, the pier was part of an ill-conceived plot to lure commercial developers to Jamaica Bay. Though the scheme never panned out, the Pier now acts as a pleasant wayside stop featuring a snack bar, full restaurant, rest rooms, a water fountain, and plenty of benches to sit back and enjoy the view.

Not too far after the route rejoins the bikeway, it passes up and over another bridge along the Belt Parkway. Though there are guardrails here, you should know that a huge puddle of water can accumulate along the bikeway just to the east; bring your snorkel! Then, not far ahead, just after the bikeway crosses yet another bridge, all of a sudden the pavement seems to disappear entirely! Instead, the bikeway becomes an ill-marked path of dirt, mud, and sand. While cyclists on mountain bikes and hybrids should be able to ride along unfettered, cyclists on road bikes will do best to dismount and walk. The "unpath" lasts for about one mile, when the pavement suddenly returns.

About one mile farther, the bikeway dips down and crosses 84th Street as the Belt Parkway crosses over the road on a bridge. Turn right onto 84th (unmarked on the bikeway) and return to St. Helen's Church and the starting point of the ride.

For Further Information

Canarsie Pier (718) 763–2202
Floyd Bennett Field (718) 338–3799
Fort Tilden/Riis Park (718) 318–4300
Gateway Park Headquarters (718) 338–3338
Jamaica Bay Wildlife Refuge (718) 318–4340

Queens
Queens Greenway

Mileage:	22
Terrain:	Rolling
Traffic:	Light to moderate (nonexistent on bikeways)
Facilities:	Rest rooms and water fountains at the Queens Museum and within most of the parks along the route.
Things to see:	Queens Museum, Flushing Meadows–Corona Park, Unisphere, New York Hall of Science, Queens Botanical Garden, Kissena Park, Cunningham Park, Alley Pond Park, Alley Pond Environmental Center, Fort Totten, Francis Lewis Park, Bowne Park

As mentioned at the beginning of Ride #5, the Brooklyn–Queens Greenway is the ambitious plan of the Neighborhood Open Space Coalition to link thirteen city parks with a series of hiking and biking trails. On this ride you will travel either on or parallel to the Greenway as it stretches from Flushing Meadows–Corona Park to Fort Totten and Clearview Park in Bayside.

Begin from the parking lot of the **Queens Museum** in **Flushing Meadows–Corona Park**. The Queens Museum, located in the New York City Building, is open daily except Monday. It features a highly detailed scale model of the city as well as many changing art exhibits.

Centrally located within Flushing Meadows–Corona Park is the **Unisphere**, symbol of the outstanding world's fair held here in 1964–65. Flushing Meadows was also the site of the equally notable 1939–40 world's fair. In fact, it was this first spectacular that led city

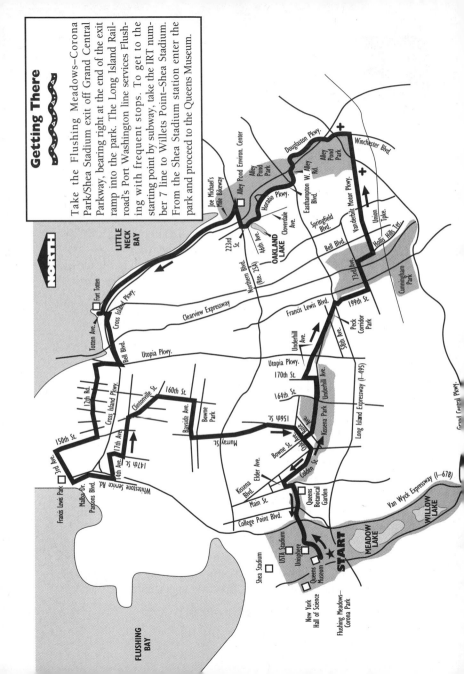

Getting There

Take the Flushing Meadows–Corona Park/Shea Stadium exit off Grand Central Parkway, bearing right at the end of the exit ramp into the park. The Long Island Railroad's Port Washington line services Flushing with frequent stops. To get to the starting point by subway, take the IRT number 7 line to Willets Point–Shea Stadium. From the Shea Stadium station enter the park and proceed to the Queens Museum.

NORTH

LITTLE NECK BAY

FLUSHING BAY

Fort Totten

Totten Ave.

Bell Blvd.

Cross Island Pkwy.

Utopia Pkwy.

12th Rd.

Cross Island Pkwy.

160th St.

Clintonville St.

150th St.

Bayside Ave.

Bowne Park

11th Ave.

14th Ave.

147th St.

Whitestone Service Rd.

3rd Ave.

Francis Lewis Park

Malba Dr.

Parsons Blvd.

Clearview Expressway

Northern Blvd. (Rte. 25A)

223rd St.

46th Ave.

Joe Michael's Mile Bikeway

Alley Pond Environ. Center

Alley Pond Park

Horatio Pkwy.

Cloverdale Ave.

OAKLAND LAKE

Douglaston Pkwy.

Alley Pond Park

Winchester Blvd.

Easthampton W. Alley Rd.

Springfield Blvd.

Vanderbilt Motor Pkwy.

Union Tpke.

Hollis Hills Ter.

Bell Blvd.

13rd Ave.

Cunningham Park

199th St.

Francis Lewis Blvd.

Peck Corridor Park

58th Ave.

Underhill Ave.

Utopia Pkwy.

170th St.

164th St.

156th St.

Kissena Park

Underhill Ave.

Long Island Expressway (I-495)

Murray St.

Bowne St.

Oak Ave.

Elder Ave.

Colden St.

Kissena Blvd.

Main St.

Queens Botanical Garden

College Point Blvd.

Van Wyck Expressway (I-678)

WILLOW LAKE

MEADOW LAKE

Grand Central Pkwy.

START

Shea Stadium

USTA Stadium

Unisphere

Queens Museum

New York Hall of Science

Flushing Meadows–Corona Park

DIREC-TIONS at a glance

0.0	Begin at Unisphere, heading east on park path.
0.3	Cross under Clearview Expressway, over College Point Boulevard, and into Kissena Park Corridor.
0.8	Exit Kissena Park Corridor; turn left onto Main Street.
0.9	Right onto Elder Avenue.
1.0	Right onto Colden Street.
1.5	Left onto Oak Avenue.
1.9	Right onto Bowne Street.
2.0	Straight across Rose Avenue and into Kissena Park.
2.4	Exit park, crossing 164th Street and continuing on Underhill Avenue.
2.7	Left onto 170th Street.
2.8	Right onto Lithonia Avenue (shortly changes name back to Underhill).
3.6	Cross 58th Avenue and switch to park path.
3.8	Cross bridge over Long Island Expressway.
3.9	Follow path toward right, walking to Peck Avenue.
4.0	Left onto Peck Avenue (becomes 199th Street).
4.4	Left onto 73rd Avenue.
4.7	Right onto Hollis Hills Terrace.
5.0	Left onto old Vanderbilt Motor Parkway.
6.6	Follow arrows from Motor Parkway through Alley Pond Park; then turn left onto Winchester Boulevard (changes name to Douglaston Parkway at top of hill).
7.7	Left onto West Alley Road.
7.9	Right onto Easthampton Boulevard.
8.6	Left onto Horatio Parkway.
8.9	Right onto Cloverdale Avenue.
9.1	Right onto 223rd Street.
9.2	Right onto Northern Boulevard (Route 25A).
9.5	After crossing Cross Island Parkway, left onto path leading to "Joe Michael's Mile" bikeway.
12.0	Bikeway ends at Fort Totten; turn left onto Totten Avenue.
12.1	Right onto Bell Boulevard.

12.8 Right onto Utopia Parkway.

13.0 Follow road straight onto Totten Street (Utopia Parkway veers to the right at the fork).

13.1 Left onto 12th Road.

14.1 Right onto 150th Street.

14.7 Left onto 3rd Avenue.

15.1 Francis Lewis Park on right.

15.2 Left onto Malba Drive, which changes names to Parsons Boulevard.

15.5 Left onto Whitestone Expressway Service Road.

15.8 Left onto 14th Avenue.

16.1 Right onto 147th Street.

16.3 Left onto 17th Avenue.

16.8 Right onto Clintonville Street.

17.3 Right onto 160th Street.

17.8 Right onto Bayside Avenue.

18.0 Bowne Park on left.

18.3 Left onto Murray Street.

19.7 Jog right onto 156th Street.

20.1 Right onto Oak Avenue.

20.5 Right onto Colden Street.

21.1 Left onto Elder Avenue.

21.2 Left onto Main Street.

21.3 Enter Kissena Park Corridor at Queens Botanical Garden. Follow path over College Point Boulevard, under Van Wyck Expressway, and back into Flushing Meadows–Corona Park to the ride's starting point.

---

parks commissioner Robert Moses to transform the area magically from an ash dump to a beautiful park setting.

The **New York Hall of Science** is located in the park at 111th Street and 48th Avenue, on the other side of Grand Central Parkway. To get there take the footbridge just south of the museum parking lot. The hall features a wide array of "user-friendly" exhibits that invite visitors to participate in the action. Displays cover a broad range of topics in all of the sciences. The hall is open Wednesday through Sunday; there is a small admission fee.

Back across Grand Central Parkway, head south on the park paths toward Meadow Lake and Willow Lake. Then circle back north along the park's eastern boundary toward Shea Stadium and the U.S. Tennis Association's stadium, home of the U.S. Open Tennis Championships. Next door to the pitch-and-putt golf course is a bicycle rental stand, which will come in handy if you are bikeless and wish to join in with the other pedalers. Call (718) 699–9598 for information.

Miles and miles of paved trails are found within Flushing Meadows–Corona Park. They, along with the attractions described above, make it easy to spend hours on a bicycle without ever leaving the park. But we must push on, for there is much to see outside of the park as well.

From the Unisphere head east along the park's paths toward the elevated Van Wyck Expressway (Interstate 678). Follow the trail under the expressway and into Kissena Park Corridor, a long, thin stretch of parkland wedged between the bustling roads of Flushing. Almost immediately after emerging from under the Van Wyck Expressway, you face one of the greatest uphill challenges of the ride as the path crosses over College Point Boulevard. The bridge is short but steep and difficult to scale if you are not prepared. The trip down the other side is invigorating but beware of bumps where the bridge meets the ground.

Continue along the bike path through Kissena Park Corridor, avoiding any sharp turns to the left or right (these lead to local roads). About 0.5 mile later, you will come to the entrance of the **Queens Botanical Garden**. Constructed in 1964, the facility features thirty-eight acres of colorful gardens and educational floral exhibits.

Past the Botanical Garden the bikeway comes to an abrupt end on Main Street. Joining traffic, continue to wind your way from Main onto Elder Avenue, Colden Street, and Oak Avenue.

Enter **Kissena Park** across from the intersection of Bowne Street and Rose Avenue. For the purpose of measuring the ride's mileage, we stayed along the northern path around Kissena Park, but you may want to tour the other bike paths as well.

Leave Kissena Park through one of its eastern exits, cross 164th Street, and continue on Underhill Avenue. After crossing 58th Avenue, shift from Underhill to the paved path in Peck Corridor Park on the right. As Underhill ends at the westbound Horace Harding Expressway (the service road adjacent to the Long Island Expressway), follow the path up and over both it and the Long Island Expressway (Interstate 495).

The path ends on the other side of the bridge, forcing riders onto the heavily traveled eastbound Horace Harding Expressway. Dismount and walk your bike, following the path to the right (against traffic). Take the first left onto Peck Avenue, which later changes its name to 199th Street. This stretch of 199th Street slices along the edge of **Cunningham Park.**

At the next intersection, turn left onto 73rd Avenue. Cross Francis Lewis Boulevard at the next intersection and continue through the park. Veer right immediately after passing under the Clearview Expressway (Interstate 295) onto Hollis Hills Terrace. Not far ahead, just before passing under a white bridge, turn left onto an unmarked paved path that heads into the woods. This is the western entrance to the old Vanderbilt Motor Parkway, which was constructed in 1906. Today few portions of its 48 original miles still exist. Fortunately, this section, which connects Cunningham Park to Alley Pond Park, has been preserved by the city as a traffic-free path to be enjoyed by cyclists, joggers, and pedestrians.

As the preserved parkway draws to a close, follow the painted arrows on the road into **Alley Pond Park.** The second largest park in Queens, Alley Pond Park boasts 623 acres of woods and meadows. At the end of the park road, turn left onto Winchester Boulevard and pass under Grand Central Parkway. The road now changes names to Douglaston Parkway and winds its way uphill, cresting in about 0.5 mile.

Although there are no paved bicycle trails to follow, the route tracks Alley Pond Park all the way to Northern Boulevard (Route 25A). On the way you will pass Oakland Lake on the left.

Crossing over the Cross Island Parkway, continue on Northern Boulevard until you come to the **Alley Pond Environmental Center.** The center, open daily, features both indoor and outdoor exhibits.

From the nature center, turn left and backtrack on Northern Boulevard for 0.25 mile. As you approach the Cross Island Parkway, turn right onto the "Joe Michael's Mile" bikeway. The bikeway parallels the northbound Cross Island Parkway and offers striking views of Little Neck Bay, Port Washington, and the distant Bronx. Along the way you will pass the Bayside Yacht Club.

The bikeway empties onto Totten Road, adjacent to the Fort Totten Army base. Fort Totten was completed in 1857, not long before the Civil War, ironically enough from a design by Robert E. Lee.

At the end of the bikeway, turn left onto Totten Road, pass under the Cross Island Parkway, then turn right onto Bell Boulevard. You'll enjoy a spectacular view of the Throgs Neck Bridge as you pedal up a small incline to the intersection with Utopia Parkway, where the route turns right. Cross above the Cross Island Parkway, then down a short hill to a fork in the road. Utopia Parkway veers off to the right, but our route goes straight onto Totten Street. Up ahead, turn left onto 12th Road (not to be confused with 12th Avenue, which lies 1 block to the north) for a pleasant trip through the residential communities of Beechurst and Whitestone.

A right turn onto 150th Street takes the route north towards Whitestone Point, while a left onto 3rd Avenue brings the ride to the foot of the Bronx-Whitestone Bridge. Lying almost directly under the bridge is a relaxing, little oasis: **Francis Lewis Park**. The park offers benches, plenty of shade trees, a rest room and water fountain, and a worm's-eye view of the bridge that connects Queens with the Bronx.

Beyond the park, pass under the access ramps to the bridge, then turn left onto Malba Drive (which changes names just ahead to Parsons Boulevard), then left again onto the Whitestone Expressway Service Road, and finally, another left onto 14th Avenue, which greets riders with a climb. Within the next mile, the route takes a right, a left, and another right as it winds through Whitestone into Flushing to end up on Clintonville Street. Clintonville holds a commercial strip that offers a deli and other important refueling stops, but also brings with it an increase in traffic. The congestion is left behind as the route veers to the right onto 160th Street, then right again onto Bayside Avenue.

Not far down Bayside on the left is **Bowne Park,** another picturesque neighborhood park. The park takes its name from John Bowne, one of the first settlers in the area. Bowne, a Quaker, arrived in 1661, only to be expelled back to Europe a year later by Governor Peter Stuyvesant, who had banned that religion. The Dutch West Indies Company, who managed the New Amsterdam colony, exonerated Bowne, allowing him to return to the New World in 1664. Today, Bowne's homestead, at the corner of 37th and Bowne Streets, stands as the oldest house in Queens. Although this ride does not visit Bowne's home, take a moment to enjoy some of the paved walks around the park's small duck pond before venturing farther along Bayside.

A left up ahead on Murray Street takes you back toward Flushing. Follow Murray across Northern Boulevard (Route 25A), then continue to the right onto 156th Street, which Murray intersects about 0.25 mile later. A right onto Oak Avenue, then another onto Colden Street, followed by left-hand turns onto Elder Avenue and Main Street retraces the route back towards the Queens Botanical Gardens. Watch for the entrance to the bikeway on the right, then follow it back into Flushing Meadows–Corona Park and the ride's starting point near the Queens Museum.

For Further Information

Flushing Meadows–Corona Park (718) 507–3117
Queens Museum (718) 592–2405
New York Hall of Science (718) 699–0005
Kissena Park Nature Center (718) 353–1047
Queens Botanical Garden (718) 886–3800
Alley Pond Environmental Center (718) 229–4000

Bronx
Van Cortlandt Park to Pelham Bay Park

Mileage:	7 (one way)
Terrain:	Mostly flat
Traffic:	Potentially heavy along portions of Mosholu and Pelham parkways, moderate elsewhere
Facilities:	Rest rooms and water fountains within Van Cortlandt and Pelham Bay Parks as well as the New York City Botanical Gardens and Bronx Zoo; several food stops along the western portion of the Bronx and Pelham Parkway
Things to see:	Van Cortlandt Park, New York Botanical Garden, Fordham University, Bronx Zoo, Pelham Bay Park

Named for Jonas Bronk, who first settled in 1639 between today's Harlem and Bronx Rivers, the Bronx presents some unusual challenges to city cyclists. In this borough of social contrasts, you will find ghetto and grandeur only a few miles apart. Some of the roads are pitted with holes that a cyclist could almost get lost in, while others are silky smooth. The Bronx is, indeed, a borough of sharp divergence.

Begin your ride in **Van Cortlandt Park,** a park rich in both natural and historical significance. Within its 1,146 acres you will find miles of roads and paths on which to cycle. One of the many sights you will find within the park is the Van Cortlandt Mansion, the oldest building in the Bronx. The mansion appears much as it did in 1748, the year it was built. Inside, each room is outfitted with authentic period furniture. Perhaps you can even imagine George Washington stand-

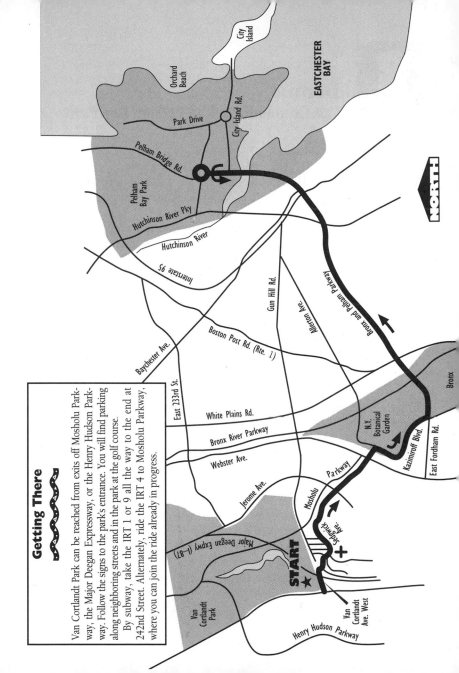

Getting There

Van Cortlandt Park can be reached from exits off Mosholu Parkway, the Major Deegan Expressway, or the Henry Hudson Parkway. Follow the signs to the park's entrance. You will find parking along neighboring streets and in the park at the golf course.

By subway, take the IRT 1 or 9 all the way to the end at 242nd Street. Alternately, ride the IRT 4 to Mosholu Parkway, where you can join the ride already in progress.

NORTH

EASTCHESTER BAY

City Island

Orchard Beach

Park Drive

City Island Rd.

Pelham Bridge Rd.

Pelham Bay Park

Hutchinson River Pky

Hutchinson River

Interstate 95

Gun Hill Rd.

Allerton Ave.

Bronx and Pelham Parkway

Baychester Ave.

Boston Post Rd. (Rte. 1)

East 233rd St.

White Plains Rd.

Bronx River Parkway

Webster Ave.

Jerome Ave.

N.Y. Botanical Garden

Kazimiroff Blvd.

Bronx

East Fordham Rd.

Mosholu Parkway

Sedgwick Ave.

Major Deegan Expwy (I-87)

START

Van Cortlandt Ave. West

Van Cortlandt Park

Henry Hudson Parkway

DIREC-TIONS at a glance

0.0	Left onto Van Cortlandt Park South from the south exit of Van Cortlandt Park.
0.3	Right onto Van Cortlandt Avenue West.
0.5	Left onto Sedgewick Avenue.
0.8	Right onto Mosholu Parkway.
1.9	Right onto Dr. Theodore Kazimiroff Boulevard.
2.8	Left onto East Fordham Road (U.S. Route 1).
3.2	Join Bronx and Pelham Parkway (see text).
6.4	Cross Hutchinson River into Pelham Bay Park.
7.1	Ride ends at traffic circle, but riders are encouraged to explore the park's many paved roads.

ing inside. He used the mansion as a meeting place during the American Revolution.

Of the many nature trails scattered throughout the park, two of the most interesting are the Aqueduct and the Old Putnam Railroad trails. The Aqueduct trail follows an aqueduct built in the 1830s to bring water to the city from the Croton reservoirs in Westchester County. Mountain bikers take note: The trail continues beyond the park's northern perimeter all the way to the Croton Dam.

The Old Putnam Railroad trail cuts the park in half. Since the last trains roared across its tracks in the late 1950s, the railroad bed has been transformed into a pleasant trail for hikers and mountain bikers.

Proceed out of the park's south exit and get ready to scale the heights of Van Cortlandt Avenue West as it heads toward Sedgewick Avenue and Mosholu Parkway. The latter, a wide, multilane road, takes you south toward Dr. Theodore Kazimiroff Boulevard and the New York Botanical Garden.

The **New York Botanical Garden** is world famous for its lush environs. Inside its rolling terrain is the Hemlock Forest, the Bronx River Gorge and Falls, and forty acres of virgin woodland. You can tiptoe through the tulips (well, not actually through, but near) daily for free. Lock your bike to the rack found near the entrance and enjoy the extraordinary grounds and buildings.

Follow Kazimiroff Boulevard counterclockwise around the gar-

PELHAM BAY PARK

City of New York   Parks & Recreation

den, passing the **Fordham University** campus on the right. At the next intersection turn left onto East Fordham Road (U. S. Route 1 north). On the corner is the entrance to the New York Zoological Park, better known as the **Bronx Zoo**. The zoo hosts more than 4,000 animals in both indoor and outdoor habitats that simulate everything from darkest Africa to the Arctic. Open daily from 10:00 A.M. until around 5:00 P.M., the park may be toured by foot, safari train, or monorail. A nominal admission fee is charged and there is an additional fee for certain attractions. It sure is easy to spend an entire day at the zoo!

Continue east on East Fordham Road (watch out for heavy traffic) and the Bronx and Pelham Bikeway. The bikeway heads east adjacent to the north side of the Bronx and Pelham Parkway. The center divider ends in 2 miles; at this point, cross back to the south side of the road to continue on the paved path.

Carefully traverse the metal-grated bridge over the Hutchinson River into **Pelham Bay Park**. Miles of trails are waiting to bring the enthusiastic cyclist around the park. For hikers there is the Thomas Pell Wildlife Refuge, a wonderful environmental center named for the area's first permanent resident from Europe. For historians there is the Bartow-Pell Mansion, completed in 1842 by Robert Bartow, a descendant of Pell. And you must take a side trip to Orchard Beach, which has been described as the "Riviera of New York."

Make a final loop around the park and cross back over Pelham Bridge. Then it's back along Pelham Parkway to Van Cortlandt Park.

For Further Information

Van Cortlandt Park (718) 543–3344
New York Botanical Garden (718) 220–8700
Bronx Zoo (718) 220–5100
Pelham Bay Park (718) 430–1890

Bronx
Riverdale, Spuyten Duyvil, and Kingsbridge

Mileage:	7
Terrain:	Very hilly
Traffic:	Light in Riverdale, moderate else-where
Facilities:	Rest rooms and water available on the campuses of Manhattan College and the College of Mount St. Vincent, as well as at Wave Hill; food stores near the corner of Fieldston Road and Mosholu Avenue, and along Irwin Avenue near West 231st Street
Things to see:	Manhattan College, Fieldston, College of Mount St. Vincent, Fonthill Castle, Wave Hill, Riverdale Park, Half Moon Overlook, Ewen Park

The Hudson River offers a beautiful backdrop for this, our most challenging ride within the five boroughs. On one hand, the ride passes through an elegant college campus, a wonderful environmental and cultural center, and thickly wooded estates that command masterful views of the river; on the other, the route follows steeply sloped hills and narrow, winding, bumpy roads. All combine to produce a truly challenging ride that will test the stamina of even the most seasoned cyclist. But don't be afraid to try this challenging ride. It is precisely this unique combination of beauty and struggle that drew us here in the first place!

Begin the ride at the intersection of Waldo Avenue, West 244th Street, and Manhattan College Parkway, right in the heart of, you guessed it, the campus of **Manhattan College**. Founded in 1853, Manhattan College offers undergraduate and graduate degree programs in a variety of subjects. The largest building on campus is Memorial Hall, a regal looking brick edifice that actually lies behind you at the ride's starting point. On either side of Memorial Hall are De La Salle Hall to the left and Miguel Hall on the right. If you have time either before or after completing the ride, you might want to tour the tree-lined campus.

From this intersection, bear right onto West 244th Street, into an exclusive community called **Fieldston**. Known for beautiful houses of stone and brick along tree-lined lanes, Fieldston features a sloping terrain that has its ups and downs as the route swerves onto Tibbett Avenue, Post Avenue, and West 253rd Street! Be forewarned that some of the roads here are very narrow and curvy, so be cautious. Although the pulse of the Bronx can be heard in the distance, the serenity of Fieldston make the urban scene seem a world away.

Climbing to the top of West 253rd Street, turn right onto Fieldston Road for a final climb up and over the Henry Hudson Parkway. Enjoy the downhill sprint to Mosholu Avenue, where you'll find a deli if all that climbing was a bit much this early on.

Continue north on Fieldston until it ends at West 262nd Street. Turn left, then take a quick right onto Tyndall Avenue and, finally another left onto West 263rd Street.

The entrance into the **College of Mount St. Vincent** lies across from the intersection of West 263rd Street and Riverdale Avenue. Now run by the Sisters of Charity, the college occupies the former estate of Edwin Forrest, a noted Shakespearean actor of the mid-nineteenth century. It was there in 1852 that Forrest constructed one of the grandest homes in the entire city. **Fonthill Castle**, a Gothic-style fortress of cut stone, is named after William Beckford's famous English castle, Fonthill Abbey. The Bronx's Fonthill features a tower, turrets, and characteristically slender windows; only lacking are a drawbridge and moat! Now home to the college's administrative offices, Fonthill Castle is open for tours by appointment. The grounds are wonderful for a slow tour by bicycle, especially during the spring.

The route continues on Riverdale Avenue to West 261st Street,

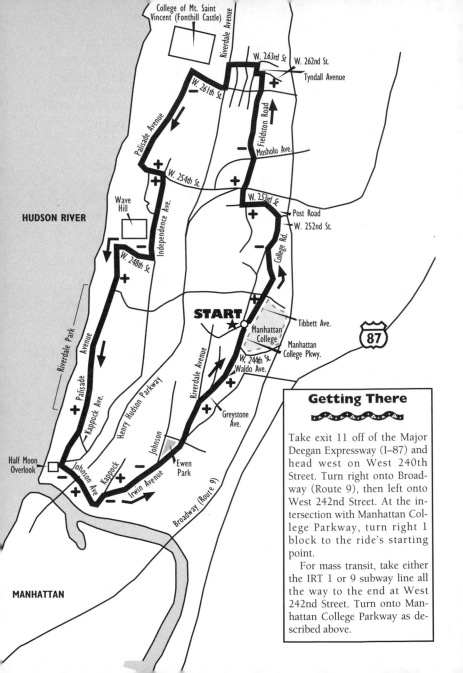

College of Mt. Saint
Vincent (Fonthill Castle)

Riverdale Avenue

W. 263rd St
W. 262nd St.
Tyndall Avenue

W. 261th St.

Palisade Avenue

Fieldston Road

Mosholu Ave.

W. 254th St.

Independence Ave.

Wave
Hill

W. 253rd St.

Post Road

W. 252nd St.

HUDSON RIVER

College Rd.

W. 248th St.

START

Tibbett Ave.

Manhattan
College

Manhattan
College Pkwy.

Riverdale Park

Riverdale Avenue

W. 244th St.
Waldo Ave.

Palisade Avenue

Kappock Ave.

Henry Hudson Parkway

Greystone
Ave.

87

Half Moon
Overlook

Johnson

Ewen
Park

Johnson Ave.

Kappock

Irwin Avenue

Broadway (Route 9)

MANHATTAN

Getting There

Take exit 11 off of the Major
Deegan Expressway (I–87) and
head west on West 240th
Street. Turn right onto Broadway (Route 9), then left onto
West 242nd Street. At the intersection with Manhattan College Parkway, turn right 1
block to the ride's starting
point.

For mass transit, take either
the IRT 1 or 9 subway line all
the way to the end at West
242nd Street. Turn onto Manhattan College Parkway as described above.

DIREC-TIONS at a glance

0.0 From the intersection of Waldo Avenue, Manhattan College Parkway, and West 244th Street, turn right onto West 244th Street.

0.1 Follow the road to the left onto Tibbett Avenue.

0.5 Right onto College Road, which changes its name just ahead to West 252nd Street.

0.6 Turn left onto Post Road.

0.7 Sharp left onto 253rd Street.

1.0 Right onto Fieldston Road.

1.7 Left onto West 262nd Street.

1.8 Right onto Tyndall Avenue.

1.9 Left onto West 263rd Street.

2.0 College of Mount St. Vincent straight ahead; route turns left onto Riverdale Avenue.

2.1 Right onto West 261st Street.

2.3 Left onto Palisade Avenue.

3.0 Left onto West 254th Street.

3.1 Right onto Independence Avenue.

3.5 Entrance to Wave Hill at West 249th Street.

3.6 Follow road to right onto West 248th Street.

3.7 Follow road to the left onto Palisade Avenue.

4.8 At intersection with Kappock Avenue, veer right to stay on Palisade Avenue.

5.1 Stay to right on Palisade Avenue (Independence veers off to left). Ahead, road makes unannounced name change to Johnson Avenue.

5.4 At stop sign with Kappock, stay to right to stay on Johnson.

5.8 Stay to right onto Irwin Avenue.

6.0 At West 231st Street, Irwin goes straight, but route veers left onto Riverdale Avenue.

6.3 Veer right onto Greystone Avenue.

6.4 At West 236th Street, veer right onto Waldo Avenue.

where it turns right and heads down a quick descent. At the base of the hill, follow the road to the left onto Palisade Avenue, a narrow roadway with a sloping shoulder. The road continues more or less downhill to West 255th Street, where it begins a ferocious ascent. With your legs aching, bear left onto West 254th Street and continue the climb to the intersection with Independence Avenue. Turning to the right, the route continues uphill until it tops off at West 252nd Street. Whew, you've just completed the ride's most difficult climb! Pause here, congratulate yourself, and rest while admiring the view of the Hudson through the trees and between the houses.

Just down the road, across from West 249th Street, is the entrance into **Wave Hill**, a unique cultural, environmental, and horticultural center. Now owned by the New York City Department of Parks, Wave Hill was once the residence of such notables as Mark Twain, Theodore Roosevelt, and Arturo Toscanini. A walk throughout its twenty-eight acres finds a wide variety of exhibits, greenhouses, botanical gardens, outdoor art shows (usually only during the summer) and even a concert hall. A $4.00 admission fee is charged except during the winter, and be forewarned that you will have to dismount and lock your bicycle at the entrance.

From Wave Hill, continue on Independence Avenue, slowly approaching the sharp right turn ahead as the route veers abruptly onto West 248th Street, plummets downhill, then shoots left back onto Palisade Avenue. The trees bordering the road on the right belong to **Riverdale Park**, a strip of woods that shield the road from the Hudson River line of the Metro North railroad.

Not long after Riverside Park ends, you will come to a fork in the road, where Palisade Avenue, and our route, veers to the right. Go slowly as you continue down and around a sharp left curve, pausing at **Half Moon Overlook** just before going under the Broadway overpass. The Overlook offers a bench for those who want to rest while drinking in the view of the Hudson, the New Jersey Palisades, and the George Washington Bridge.

Crossing under the Broadway overpass, the road makes an unannounced name change to Johnson Avenue, the neighborhood to Spuyten Duyvil. Stay to the right up ahead at the split with Kappock Street to stay on Johnson Avenue. At the following intersection, however, stay to the right to change onto Irwin Avenue. A block later, a small neighborhood park, **Ewen Park**, offers thirsty riders a water fountain.

Just beyond Ewen Park, the road splits again, with Irwin forking to the right and Riverdale Avenue (and our route) to the left. Continue 1 block up (yes, unfortunately, uphill) Riverdale, veering to the right onto Greystone Avenue for 1 block, then another right onto Waldo Avenue. Manhattan College and the ride's beginning lie less than half a mile up the road.

For Further Information

Manhattan College (718) 862–8000
Fonthill Castle (718) 405–3345
Wave Hill (718) 549–2055

Staten Island
Grymes Hill to Snug Harbor

Mileage:	8
Terrain:	Hilly
Traffic:	Moderate
Facilities:	Rest rooms and water fountains within Clove Lakes Park, Staten Island Zoo, Snug Harbor Cultural Center, and Silver Lake State Park; food stops along Victory Boulevard and Broadway
Things to see:	Wagner College, Clove Lakes Park, Staten Island Zoo, Snug Harbor Cultural Center, Silver Lake Park

Although it has grown considerably since the opening of the Verrazano-Narrows Bridge in 1964, Staten Island remains the most rural of the city's five boroughs. Its pleasant blend of big-city and suburban charms allows city cyclists to enjoy the best of both worlds right in their own backyards.

Begin along Howard Avenue atop Grymes Hill, the second highest hill on Staten Island. Commanding center stage amid the beautiful homes and numerous garden apartments on Grymes Hill is **Wagner College**. The Wagner campus is noted for its countrylike beauty and, in sharp contrast, its commanding view of lower Manhattan, the Verrazano-Narrows Bridge, Brooklyn, and New York Harbor. We are both especially fond of Wagner College. It was here, as undergraduate students, that we first met on a snowy night in January 1978 (no, we were *not* riding bicycles at the time).

Coast down Grymes Hill on Howard Avenue. Don't build up too

much speed on the way down, since you must stop at the bottom and turn right onto Clove Road. You will soon arrive at the four-way intersection at Clove and Victory Boulevard. Turn left onto Victory; then, just ahead on the right, steer into **Clove Lakes Park**. Actually, there are several paved paths into the park from which you may choose. You might prefer to ride along the shore of Clove Lake itself or to cycle through the park's adjacent woodlands. And if you just happen to have a pair of ice skates with you, there is always the park's ice rink.

Exiting from Clove Lakes Park, turn right onto Martling Avenue and right again onto Clove Road. Watch for the **Staten Island Zoo** across from the intersection between Martling and Clove Road. The zoo has something for everyone. Outside is a pony track and barn and exhibits featuring flamingos, otters, raccoons, and porcupines. Indoor displays include a marvelous aquarium, a serpentarium, African savannah, and a tropical rain forest. For kids a petting zoo lets everyone feed goats and watch ducks dive into their pond. The zoo is open daily from 10:00 A.M. to 4:45 P.M., with entrances on both Clove Road and Broadway. A small admission fee is charged.

The route turns left onto Glenwood Place, then left again onto Broadway. Broadway will lead you all the way to Richmond Terrace and the Kill Van Kull, a narrow strip of water that marks the north shore of Staten Island. Turn right onto Richmond Terrace and continue for 0.7 mile, where you will meet Snug Harbor Road and the **Snug Harbor Cultural Center** on the right. Founded in 1801, Snug Harbor was the nation's first maritime hospital and home for retired sailors. Today, its twenty-eight buildings and eighty acres comprise a wonderful park setting.

Back on Richmond Terrace the route winds inland along Lafayette, Brighton, and Castleton Avenues. Bordering Forest Avenue to the south is **Silver Lake Park**, another pleasant city park for cycling. Follow Silver Lake Park Road past the lake itself. For a beautiful view, shoot off onto the path that crosses the dam in the middle of Silver Lake.

Emerging from the other side of the park, turn left onto Victory Boulevard, then right onto Theresa Place for the final climb up Grymes Hill. Back on Howard Avenue you will pass many regal homes, as well as the Staten Island campus of Saint John's University.

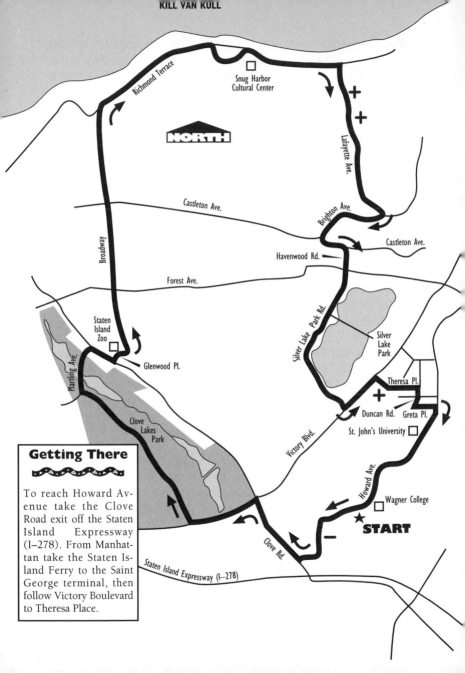

KILL VAN KULL

Richmond Terrace

Snug Harbor
Cultural Center

NORTH

Lafayette Ave.

Castleton Ave.

Broadway

Brighton Ave.

Castleton Ave.

Havenwood Rd.

Forest Ave.

Silver Lake Park Rd.

Staten
Island
Zoo

Silver
Lake
Park

Glenwood Pl.

Martling Ave.

Theresa Pl.

Clove
Lakes
Park

Victory Blvd.

Duncan Rd.   Greta Pl.

St. John's University

Howard Ave.

Getting There

To reach Howard Avenue take the Clove Road exit off the Staten Island Expressway (I–278). From Manhattan take the Staten Island Ferry to the Saint George terminal, then follow Victory Boulevard to Theresa Place.

Clove Rd.

Staten Island Expressway (I–278)

Wagner College

★ **START**

DIREC-TIONS at a glance

0.0	Begin on Howard Avenue across from Wagner College.
0.3	Right onto Clove Road.
0.7	Left onto Victory Boulevard.
1.0	Right into Clove Lakes Park.
1.4	Right onto Martling Avenue.

1.6	Right onto Clove Road.
1.7	Left onto Glenwood Place.
1.8	Left onto Broadway.
2.9	Right onto Richmond Terrace.
3.3	Stay to the left on Richmond Terrace.
4.2	Right onto Lafayette Avenue.
4.9	Right onto Brighton Avenue.
5.2	Left onto Castleton Avenue.
5.3	Right onto Havenwood Street.
5.4	Straight into Silver Lake Park Road.
6.2	Left onto Victory Boulevard.
6.3	Right onto Theresa Place.
6.6	Right onto Duncan Road.
6.8	Left onto Greta Place.
6.9	Right onto Howard Avenue.
7.5	Back at Wagner College.

Once past Saint John's, continue on Howard back to the Wagner College campus.

For Further Information

Wagner College (718) 390–3100
Clove Lakes Park (718) 390–8031
Staten Island Zoo (718) 442–3101
Snug Harbor Cultural Center (718) 448–2500
Silver Lake Park (718) 816–5466

Staten Island
Great Kills to South Beach and Todt Hill

Mileage:	20
Terrain:	Flat, except for Todt Hill
Traffic:	Moderate
Facilities:	Rest rooms and water fountains within Great Kills Park, High Rock Conservation Center, and Richmondtown Restoration; food stops available along West Fingerboard Road, Richmond Road, and Hylan Boulevard
Things to see:	Great Kills Park, Richmondtown Restoration, Midland Beach, South Beach, Todt Hill, High Rock Conservation Center

The eastern shore of Staten Island has something for every bicyclist. For the seasoned pedaler there are challenging uphill climbs, while for the casual rider there are long, flat expanses with little or no traffic. On this ride you will experience both.

The tour opens with a visit to **Great Kills Park**, part of the Gateway National Recreation Area. Gateway is made up of four park units along the coast adjacent to New York Harbor. Great Kills Park is formed from a peninsula jutting out into Lower New York Bay. Once the site of an Algonquin Indian village, the land was purchased in 1860 by one John Crooke. Crooke, a reclusive mining engineer and naturalist, made his home at the peninsula's tip, now known as Crooke's Point. New York City purchased the land in 1929 and opened Great Kills Park twenty years later. In 1974 park jurisdiction was transferred to the National Park Service, which has maintained it ever since.

The park's natural habitat is home to many coastal plants and animals. Along some of the footpaths you will find seaside goldenrod, bayberry, prickly pear, and several other unique flora. Hiding among the dunes and gullies are squirrels, rabbits, turtles, ring-necked pheasants, and many other small animals. If you choose to venture along one of the trails, please observe the park rule that bicycles are strictly prohibited.

Leave the park along its lone entrance road. Cross Hylan Boulevard and join Buffalo Street. Follow Buffalo until it ends at the Staten Island Rapid Transit tracks; then take a left onto South Railroad Avenue. In 3 blocks turn right on Justin Avenue. Follow Justin as it passes under the orange railroad bridge and all the way to Amboy Road; turn right. Homes line the eastern side of Amboy Road, while a large cemetery takes up a good part of the other side.

About 0.25 mile after the cemetery ends, take a left onto Clarke Avenue. Though it begins on a commercial note, Clarke quickly changes into a residential road with a suburban flavor.

Just before Clarke ends at Arthur Kill Road, turn right into **Richmondtown Restoration.** Richmondtown re-creates the Staten Island of colonial days. Throughout its 100 acres the restoration features fourteen buildings outfitted with period furnishings and informative exhibits. Guides perform tasks that were once part of everyday life on the island. Be sure to stop at the Staten Island Historical Society's museum and store, located at 441 Clarke Avenue. The store offers a wide range of unique gifts and souvenirs, from pewter jewelry to teddy bears. The restoration is open Wednesday through Sunday, as well as Monday holidays, and there is an admission charge. Allow between one and two hours for a complete tour.

Leave Richmondtown on Richmond Road heading east. Two confusing intersections lie ahead. As Richmond Road temporarily veers to the left, continue straight on Morley Avenue for 0.2 mile, then rejoin Richmond. The second uncertain junction occurs at the T intersection with Amboy Road. As Amboy peels off to the right, follow the green-and-white BIKE ROUTE sign toward the left to stay on Richmond.

Entering the Grant City part of the island, turn right onto one-way Midland Avenue. After crossing Hylan Boulevard, Midland be-

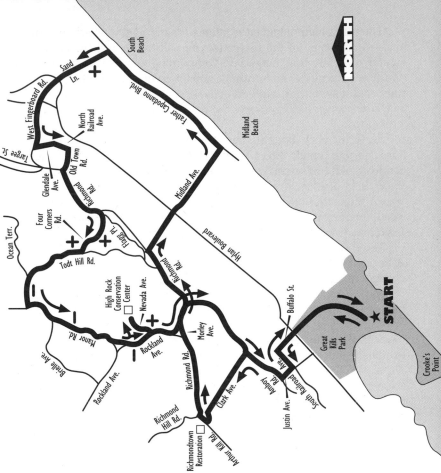

NORTH

South Beach

Sand Ln.

West Fingerboard Rd.

Father Capodanno Blvd.

North Railroad Ave.

Targee St.

Glendale Ave.

Old Town Rd.

Richmond Rd.

Midland Ave.

Midland Beach

Ocean Terr.

Four Corners Rd.

Flagg Pl.

Todt Hill Rd.

High Rock Conservation Center

Nevada Ave.

Richmond Rd.

Hylan Boulevard

Manor Rd.

Rockland Ave.

Morley Ave.

Buffalo St.

Bfielle Ave.

Rockland Ave.

Richmond Rd.

Clark Ave.

Amboy Rd.

Great Kills Park

START

Richmond Hill Rd.

Richmondtown Restoration

Arthur Kill Rd.

Justin Ave.

South Railroad Ave.

Crooke's Point

Getting There

Take the Hylan Boulevard exit off the Staten Island Expressway (I-278) just before the Verrazano Bridge. Travel south on Hylan for about 5 miles to the park's entrance on the left.

By mass transit, take the Staten Island Rapid Transit line from the ferry terminal to the Great Kills Station, adjacent to the ride's start.

0.0   Begin at Great Kills Park visitors' center.
1.0   Cross Hylan Boulevard onto Buffalo Street.
1.3   Left onto South Railroad Avenue.
1.5   Right onto Justin Avenue.
1.7   Right onto Amboy Road.
2.2   Left onto Clarke Avenue.

3.1   Right onto Arthur Kill Road.
3.3   Right onto Richmond Road.
4.3   Straight onto Morley Avenue.
4.5   Straight onto Richmond Road.
4.7   Left to stay on Richmond Road.
5.5   Right onto Midland Avenue.
6.8   Left onto Father Capodanno Boulevard.
8.6   Left onto Sand Lane.
9.3   Straight onto West Fingerboard Road.
10.2   Left onto Glendale Avenue.
10.4   Straight onto North Railroad Avenue.
10.6   Right onto Old Town Road.
10.9   Left onto Richmond Road.
11.4   Right onto Four Corners Road. Continue to the right at the stop sign just ahead to stay on Four Corners Road.
12.1   Right onto Todt Hill Road.
12.8   Left onto Ocean Terrace.
13.1   Left onto Manor Road.
14.2   Left onto Rockland Avenue.
14.8   Left onto Nevada Avenue to end; turn around.
16.2   Left back onto Rockland Avenue.
16.4   Left onto Richmond Road.
16.8   Right onto Amboy Road.
18.3   Left onto Justin Avenue.
18.4   Left onto South Railroad Avenue.
18.6   Right onto Buffalo Street.
18.9   Straight into Great Kills Park.
19.9   Return to visitors' center.

comes a two-way road featuring a separate bike lane on the right. Be watchful of any cars parked between the bike lane and the curb. Follow Midland until it ends at Father Capodanno Boulevard. Turn left and join the adjacent bikeway. Paralleling the road on the right are **Midland Beach** and **South Beach,** both with great views of Brooklyn across the harbor, with Coney Island on the right, Fort Hamilton straight ahead, and the Verrazano-Narrows Bridge off to the left.

Just before the end of the bikeway, turn left onto Sand Lane and begin the climb toward Hylan Boulevard. Cross Hylan to join West Fingerboard Road. After traversing the railroad tracks, turn left onto Glendale Avenue. Continue onto North Railroad Avenue until it ends at Old Town Road. Take a right onto Old Town and proceed to its end at Richmond Road. Turning left onto Richmond, get ready to face one of the most challenging parts of this ride—challenging not because of any great hills but because it's a narrow, bumpy, heavily traveled road. Exercise extreme caution as you pedal along this stretch.

Turn right onto Four Corners Road and start the ascent up **Todt Hill**—and we do mean up! Todt Hill rises more than 400 feet above sea level, making it the second highest point on the east coast. (If you want to avoid the climb, continue on Richmond and pick up the route ahead at Amboy Road.) When Four Corners Road ends, take a right onto Todt Hill Road to continue the climb toward the peak.

Veer left onto Ocean Terrace, followed by another left onto Manor Road to begin the descent of Todt Hill. Up ahead the road forks, with Manor continuing to the right. You want to stay to the left to join Rockland Avenue. Don't build up too much speed, because you'll turn left again just ahead.

That left puts you on Nevada Avenue, heading up toward **High Rock Conservation Center.** That's right, to get to the nature center, you have to climb back up part of Todt Hill. Sorry about that! But the trip is worth it, because High Rock, which the U.S. Department of the Interior has designated a National Environmental Education Landmark, is a one-of-a-kind place on Staten Island. Throughout its seventy-two acres of rich forest, you will find a number of hiking trails, interpretive exhibits, and a unique garden for the blind. The center is open daily from 9:00 A.M. to 5:00 P.M. There is no charge for admission.

Back on Rockland Avenue, continue to its end at Richmond Road. Turn right onto Amboy Road. Stay on Amboy until you arrive back at Justin Avenue. A left onto Justin, another left onto South Railroad Avenue, and a right onto Buffalo return you to Hylan Boulevard and, across the way, Great Kills Park.

For Further Information

Great Kills Park (718) 351–8700
Richmondtown Restoration (718) 351–1617
High Rock Conservation Center (718) 667–6042

Nassau County, Long Island

Bethpage Bikeway and Beyond

Mileage: 26
Terrain: Flat on bikeway, rolling elsewhere
Traffic: Light (nonexistent on bikeway)
Facilities: Rest rooms and water fountains in Bethpage State Park, Old Bethpage Village Restoration, and Battle Row Campground; snack bars at the state park and restoration in season
Things to see: Massapequa Preserve, Bethpage State Park, Quaker Cemetery, Battle Row Park (camping optional), Old Bethpage Village Restoration

June 30, 1899 was an important date in Long Island bicycling history. That was the day that Brooklyn's Charles Murphy accepted the challenge to pedal 1 mile in one minute. Murphy rode on a special wooden track laid between the rails of the Long Island Railroad stretching between Bethpage and Babylon. He chose to follow a specially outfitted train designed to act as a windbreak. In the end Murphy had cycled the mile in 57.8 seconds, setting a record that held for forty years.

While we may admire Murphy's great accomplishment, we are certainly not out to challenge it. Our ride into and through the area will be at a much more leisurely pace. The Long Island Railroad does, however, offer a convenient starting point. Park at the Massapequa railroad station, an ideal place to disembark. Look for the BETHPAGE BIKEWAY signs beyond the station's eastern end. The bikeway offers a pleasant, traffic-free ride between Massapequa and Bethpage State Park. (Just watch out for other cyclists, pedestrians, and the occasional dog.) First, why not stop at a local deli and pick up something for lunch, since the bikeway ends at the state park's picnic area?

The first half of Bethpage Bikeway meanders through **Massapequa Preserve**. This nature lover's oasis is wedged between Sunrise Highway and the Southern State Parkway. The bikeway rolls through the preserve along the west bank of a small pond, where children of all ages go fishing.

The path continues, following a stream to the north. Along the way small dams create ponds and marshes that abound with birds and waterfowl. During the spring and summer, wildflowers blossom throughout the preserve, adding color to the land and a delightful scent to the air.

As Massapequa Preserve ends, the bikeway continues northward alongside Bethpage State Parkway. The only hill you will encounter before entering **Bethpage State Park** is the bridge up and over the Southern State Parkway; it is short but steep. Note that while the path remains separated from the road, it does cross each entrance and exit ramp. Riders *must* stop at each intersection and yield the right-of-way to automobile traffic. Be careful.

Once inside the park the bikeway continues all the way to the picnic area. This calls for lunch. Afterward, explore some of the park on foot. You will find ball fields and golf courses galore throughout its 1,475 acres.

Leave the park the same way you entered it. At the Central Avenue exit on the northbound side of Bethpage Parkway, turn left and carefully ride (or walk) to the ramp's end, where you will turn left. Keep turning to the left, winding from Central onto Quaker Meetinghouse Road. At the top of a rather long hill on Quaker Meetinghouse Road is another entrance into Bethpage Park. Inside are tennis courts and a clubhouse.

Across from the park entrance is the **Quaker Cemetery**. At the east end of the cemetery is the Quaker meetinghouse itself. While it is a new construction, a state historical marker indicates that meetings have been held at the site since 1698.

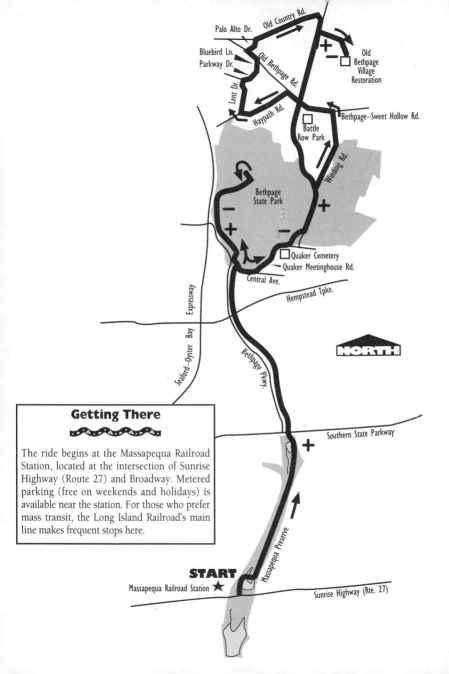

Palo Alto Dr.
Old Country Rd.

Bluebird Ln.
Parkway Dr.
Old Bethpage Rd.

Old Bethpage Village Restoration

Lent Dr.

Haypath Rd.

Bethpage—Sweet Hollow Rd.

Battle Row Park

Winding Rd.

Bethpage State Park

Quaker Cemetery
Quaker Meetinghouse Rd.

Central Ave.

Hempstead Tpke.

Seaford—Oyster Bay Expressway

NORTH

Bethpage Pkwy.

Southern State Parkway

Getting There

The ride begins at the Massapequa Railroad Station, located at the intersection of Sunrise Highway (Route 27) and Broadway. Metered parking (free on weekends and holidays) is available near the station. For those who prefer mass transit, the Long Island Railroad's main line makes frequent stops here.

Massapequa Preserve

START
Massapequa Railroad Station ★

Sunrise Highway (Rte. 27)

DIRECTIONS at a glance

0.0 Head north from the Massapequa Railroad Station on Bethpage Bikeway.

6.6 Bikeway ends at Bethpage State Park picnic area. Turn around.

8.3 Left onto exit ramp toward Central Avenue.

8.4 Left onto Central Avenue.

8.8 Left onto Quaker Meetinghouse Road.

9.5 Left onto Round Swamp Road.

10.1 Right onto Winding Road.

11.1 Left onto Bethpage–Sweet Hollow Road.

11.6 Straight across Round Swamp Road onto Old Bethpage Road.

11.8 Left onto Haypath Road.

12.6 Right onto Lent Drive.

13.2 Right onto Parkway Drive (Clearwater comes in from left).

13.5 Right onto Bluebird Lane.

13.6 Left onto Old Bethpage Road.

13.8 Right onto Palo Alto Drive.

14.0 Right onto Old Country Road.

15.0 Right onto Round Swamp Road.

15.1 Left into Old Bethpage Village Restoration. To return, turn left out of the restoration exit onto Round Swamp Road.

18.1 Right onto Quaker Meetinghouse Road.

18.5 Right onto Central Avenue.

18.9 Right onto northbound entrance ramp to Bethpage Parkway.

19.0 Left onto southbound bikeway (stay off the parkway!).

25.7 Welcome back to the Massapequa railroad station.

Bear right at the fork up ahead for Winding Road. Do you smell smoke? If so, don't worry—it's just the Nassau County Fire Service Academy, located up ahead on the left. From the looks of a couple of the buildings on the academy's grounds, they have been doing quite a bit of training recently! Farther along, as the road curves to the left, watch for truck traffic that may be entering. At the end of Winding Road, turn left onto Bethpage–Sweet Hollow Road.

Just ahead on the left, toward the top of a slow climb, don't be surprised if you see trailers, campers, and motor homes turning down Claremont Road. They're staying at **Battle Row Campground**, the only campground in Nassau county. More adventurous readers, consider turning this ride into an overnighter. Bicycle camping is a unique experience, one that every cyclist should try at least once. But be sure to telephone ahead for reservations, as Battle Row does not permit walk-ins.

Continue straight across the intersection with Round Swamp Road onto Old Bethpage Road. At the next traffic light, turn left onto Haypath Road and continue for just under a mile to Lent Drive, where the route turns right. Haypath and Lent cut through a quiet, tree-lined neighborhood of residential homes that is great for casual cycling. At the stop sign midway through the development, veer to the right onto Parkway Drive, followed by a right onto Bluebird Lane a little farther along. Bluebird ends quickly at Old Bethpage Road, where the route turns left. Old Bethpage is a busy thoroughfare, but fortunately, the route swings off in 3 blocks onto Palo Alto Drive. Just ahead, around a bend, you'll have to cut onto the sidewalk to pedal around a locked gate across the road that separates the houses along Palo Alto from a condominium complex that lies on the other side. Once on the other side of the gate, be watchful for three speed bumps that not only slow cars, but also give cyclists quite a jolt.

Turn right onto Old Country Road and pedal along for about one mile to the intersection with Round Swamp Road. Though heavily trafficked, Old Country Road offers a wide shoulder for safe cycling. At the fork in the road, bear right onto Round Swamp Road.

Only about 0.25 mile after joining Round Swamp, watch on the left for **Old Bethpage Village**. Follow the 0.5-mile-long entrance road into the restoration and secure your bike to one of the racks near the reception center. Inside are exhibits, a gift shop, and a cafeteria. Entering the village itself, you will feel as though you have passed through a time warp. Old Bethpage Village is an authentic re-creation

78

of a nineteenth-century farming community, with the oldest building dating to 1765. All structures have been moved to the restoration from their original sites throughout Long Island.

Among the more interesting buildings in the village are the general store, the country inn, and the farm. Guides dressed in clothing of the period are eager to tell visitors about each of the village's forty-five buildings scattered over the 200-acre site. You should allow at least two hours to tour Old Bethpage Village, so plan your day accordingly.

The return trip follows Round Swamp Road back toward Bethpage State Park. To get back on the bikeway, carefully ride (or walk) down the northbound entrance ramp to Bethpage Parkway off Central Avenue. Just before the ramp merges onto the parkway, turn left at the BIKE ROUTE sign for the return trip to the Massapequa Railroad Station.

For Further Information

Bethpage State Park (516) 249–0701
Old Bethpage Village (516) 420–5280
Battle Row Campground (516) 293–7120

Suffolk County, Long Island
Greenlawn–Huntington

Mileage:	13
Terrain:	Rolling
Traffic:	Moderate near the center of Huntington; light elsewhere
Facilities:	Rest rooms at the Greenlawn Railroad Station and Hecksher Park—the latter also has water fountains; food stops along New York Avenue (Route 110), Mill Dam Road, and West Shore Road
Things to see	Nathan Hale marker, Mill Dam Park, Hecksher Museum and Park, the Arsenal

Each July, the Huntington Bicycle Club sponsors the Gold Coast Tour, an organized ride that attracts more than a hundred of the area's cyclists. Following routes that vary in length from 25 miles to 100 miles, Gold Coast riders meander through Suffolk and Nassau Counties, passing some of the most magnificent harbor views that the island's historic north shore has to offer. This route, beginning in Greenlawn, follows some portions of the Gold Coast's route as it winds its way northward toward Huntington Bay. In fact, keep an eye out on the roads for painted arrows—cues for the Gold Coast riders to follow.

Begin the ride at the Greenlawn Railroad Station, adjacent to Broadway and Boulevard Avenue. Proceed straight across Broadway onto Smith Street. At the end of Smith, at a rather strangely constructed four-way intersection between Smith, Dunlop Road, and Tilden Lane, take a hard right onto Tilden.

At the end of Tilden, turn left onto Old Field Road. Enjoy a brief downhill run past Old Field Middle School to the end of the road, where the route turns right onto Greenlawn Road. Follow Greenlawn as it winds downhill toward Huntington. As the route passes J. Taylor Finley Junior High School on the left, just before Greenlawn ends, take a right onto Loma Place, then another quick right onto East Main Street (Route 25A). Though this latter road is littered with cars, the ride leaves it at the intersection with Huntington Bay Road, just 0.1 mile ahead on the left at the traffic light. Just be careful as you cross the road.

Huntington Bay Road offers cyclists a wonderful tree-lined welcome to Huntington Bay. Start by heading down Gallows Hill. According to the historical marker along the roadside, this was the site where two American martyrs were hanged by the British during the Revolutionary War.

Continue straight at the four-way intersection with Cove Road, until you come to a second four-way stop with Bay Avenue. Turn left onto the rutted concrete road but then quickly take the next right onto Locust Lane. Once up a small climb at the beginning, Locust flattens out, passing some lovely homes along the way. As Locust begins to dip down, turn left onto Sydney Road. As the map shows, wind your way from Sydney, turning left onto Taylor Road, then right onto Cedar Lane. Cedar is very bumpy and narrow as it goes downhill, so take it slowly. Along the way, you'll pass a unique driveway that has a huge boulder set squarely in its middle. It must be quite a conversation starter with the neighbors. At the end of Cedar, turn left onto Vineyard Road. Up ahead, Vineyard veers to the left, but our bike route continues straight up Kaiser Hill Road, the ride's steepest climb.

Turn right onto Bay Avenue for the sprint out to Sandy Point. Again, enjoy the view of the sculpted homes and lawns that line the peaceful streets in this exclusive neighborhood. From Bay, loop around the point on Hecksher Drive, Woodland Drive, and finally Wincoma Drive. Though the road remains the same, Win-

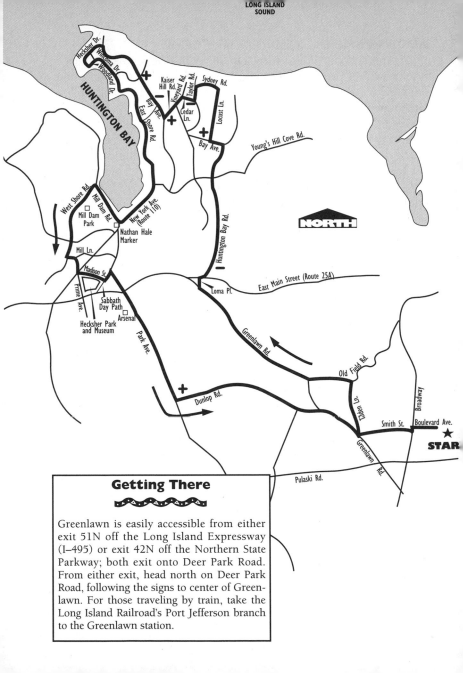

LONG ISLAND
SOUND

Hecksher Dr.

Winkoma Dr.

Woodland Dr.

HUNTINGTON BAY

Bay Ave.

East Shore Rd.

Kaiser Hill Rd.

Vineyard Rd.

Taylor Rd.

Sydney Rd.

Cedar Ln.

Locust Ln.

Bay Ave.

Young's Hill Cove Rd.

West Shore Rd.

Mill Dam Park

Mill Dam Rd.

New York Ave. (Route 110)

Nathan Hale Marker

Huntington Bay Rd.

NORTH

Mill Ln.

Madison St.

Prime Ave.

Sabbath Day Path

Arsenal

Hecksher Park and Museum

Park Ave.

Loma Pl.

East Main Street (Route 25A)

Greenlawn Rd.

Old Field Rd.

Broadway

Tilden Ln.

Dunlop Rd.

Smith St.

Boulevard Ave.

★ **STAR**

Greenlawn Rd.

Pulaski Rd.

Getting There

Greenlawn is easily accessible from either exit 51N off the Long Island Expressway (I–495) or exit 42N off the Northern State Parkway; both exit onto Deer Park Road. From either exit, head north on Deer Park Road, following the signs to center of Greenlawn. For those traveling by train, take the Long Island Railroad's Port Jefferson branch to the Greenlawn station.

DIREC-TIONS at a glance

0.0	Begin from the north parking lot of the Green lawn Railroad Station, leaving via the Boulevard Avenue exit.
0.1	Jog left across Broadway onto Smith Street.
0.5	Make a hard right onto Tilden Lane.
1.0	Turn left onto Old Field Road.
1.3	At the fork, turn right onto Greenlawn Road.
2.6	Bear right onto Loma Place.
2.7	Turn right onto East Main Street (Route 25A).
2.8	Turn left onto Huntington Bay Road.
3.9	Turn left onto Bay Avenue.
4.0	Turn right onto Locust Lane.
4.5	Turn left onto Sydney Road.
4.7	Turn left onto Taylor Road.
4.8	Turn right onto Cedar Lane.
4.9	Turn left onto Vineyard Road.
5.0	Continue straight onto Kaiser Hill Road.
5.2	Turn right onto Bay Avenue.
6.1	Follow Bay Avenue to the left as it turns into Hecksher Drive.
6.4	At the triangular island, bear left onto Woodland Drive.
6.5	Stay to the right on Woodland.
6.6	Bear right onto Wincoma Drive, which changes up ahead to East Shore Road.
7.9	Continue as the road changes into New York Avenue (Route 110).
8.2	Turn right onto Mill Dam Road.
8.6	Turn left onto West Shore Road.
9.3	Turn left onto Mill Lane.
9.4	Veer to the right on Prime Avenue.
9.5	Crossing New York Avenue, bear left onto Madison Street.
9.8	Turn left onto Sabbath Day Path.
9.9	Turn right onto Park Avenue.
11.0	Turn left onto Dunlop Road.
12.3	Turn right at the stop sign onto Greenlawn Road.
12.7	Turn left onto Smith Street.
13.2	Zigzag to the left across Broadway onto Boulevard Avenue.
13.3	Turn right into the Greenlawn railroad parking lot.

coma's name changes to East Shore Road just before it passes Huntington Yacht Club on the right. A little farther down, a small park on the same side of the road greets riders who may want to take a break and admire the harbor view.

Not long after passing Ketewomoke Yacht Club, the road changes names once again, becoming New York Avenue (State Route 110). This time the change is noticeable, as the paved surface goes from smooth blacktop to less-than-smooth concrete. Congestion is also likely to increase, as the surroundings become more commercial.

Turn right onto Mill Dam Road, but before proceeding, pause for a moment at the stone monument to the Revolutionary War patriot **Nathan Hale**. Born in Coventry, Connecticut, Hale graduated from Yale University in 1773 and enlisted in the 7th Connecticut Regiment two years later. Promoted to the rank of captain, he volunteered to be an American spy a year later. Following his crossing of Long Island Sound, Hale was discovered by the British and taken prisoner. Shortly before being hanged near this spot, Hale uttered those immortal words, "I only regret that I have but one life to lose for my country."

As Mill Dam Road ends at a T intersection with West Shore Road, you may want to pause to take in the sights at either **Mill Dam Park** on the left, or the boat marina on the right. (Or, if you feel like going a little farther than our ride here, take a right as the Gold Coast cyclists would, and follow West Shore Road along the opposite bank of Huntington Harbor. From here, you can also pursue Ride #7 in *Short Bike Rides on Long Island* for a trip to Lloyd Neck and Cold Spring Harbor.)

Turn left onto West Shore Road. Be careful as the traffic gets a little heavier as you pass a couple of small shopping centers on either side of the road. As they end, turn left onto Mill Lane. As Mill forks, follow Prime Avenue to the right. Continue on Prime Avenue across New York Avenue. While the route turns left onto Madison, you might want to take a moment to visit the **Hecksher Museum** located farther down Prime Avenue on the right. The museum is the only art museum on Long Island with exhibitions and collections spanning 500 years of western art. The museum's permanent collection also spotlights works by noted contemporary American artists, many of whom live on Long Island. The Hecksher Museum is open Tuesday through Friday from 10:00 A.M. to 5:00 P.M. and weekends from 1:00 to 5:00 P.M. A voluntary entrance donation fee of $2.00 is suggested.

Passing **Hecksher Park** on the right as you continue down Madison Street, don't be surprised if you see some radio-controlled sailboats sailing in among the ducks in the park's pond. Sailboat racing is a popular activity in the park on spring, summer, and fall afternoons. At the end of Madison, turn left onto Sabbath Day Path, then right onto Park Avenue, circling an extension of Hecksher Park noted for its unusual "sleeping tree" (at least that's how it strikes us).

Cross Main Street and continue on Park. Up ahead, pass the **Arsenal** on the right, a building dating to colonial times when it was used to store munitions. Park then begins a slow climb to the left-hand intersection with Dunlop Road. Downshift into a lower gear and climb the ride's longest hill (about 0.9 mile) on your way back toward Greenlawn. At the stop sign ahead, follow Greenlawn Road more or less to the right. Turn left down Smith Street and follow it back into the village of Greenlawn where the ride began.

For Further Information

Hecksher Museum (516) 351–3250

Suffolk County, Long Island
Smithtown

Mileage:	23
Terrain:	Hilly
Traffic:	Moderate on Route 25, light elsewhere
Facilities:	Food stops available at the ride's starting point as well as at the corner of Route 25A and Bread and Cheese Hollow Road; rest rooms and water fountains within Sunken Meadow State Park and Blydenburgh County Park
Things to see:	Smithtown Historical District, Kings Park Bluff, Sunken Meadow State Park, Smithtown Bull, Blydenburgh County Par, Miller's Pond Park

Surrounding the Nissequogue River on the north shore of western Suffolk County is the village of Smithtown. Smithtown exemplifies much of modern-day Long Island—a nice blend of contemporary and historical flavors nestled in a pleasant suburban setting.

Just east of the town's center (also known as the Village of the Branch) on the north side of Main Street (Route 25) are a number of buildings that date back to the town's beginnings. Among the buildings found in the **Smithtown Historical District** are the Caleb Smith House (1819), open daily except Sunday and featuring historic exhibits; the Epenetus Smith Tavern (1740); the J. Lawrence Smith Homestead (circa 1750); and the Franklin Arthur Farm (1740), complete with carriage house, barn, and smokehouse. All are maintained by the Smithtown Historical Society.

Our route heads out of the Village of the Branch on Landing Avenue. The town's bustling commercial center quickly gives way to a quiet tree-lined street of stately homes. Crossing Edgewood Avenue, the route plunges toward its first crossing of the Nissequogue. On the right is Landing Avenue Park, featuring a playground and a small picnic area. It is not unusual to spot a canoe or a kayak maneuvering downriver here, especially on warmer weekends.

Farther down Landing Avenue on the right, just before the ride's first big climb, is the Smithtown Landing Methodist Church. Wandering through the churchyard, you will find stones dating back to the 1830s. Though not used for weekly services, the church still hosts special gatherings.

Continuing northward, the road climbs until it crests at the Smithtown Landing Country Club. Open to town residents only, the club boasts a fine golf course, a clubhouse, and three outdoor pools.

As quickly as it rose, Landing Avenue drops toward its northern end, where the ride takes a left and two rights to end up on Riviera Drive. You will soon find yourself riding along the western shore of the Nissequogue's mouth, a lovely example of a saltwater marshland populated by many different waterfowl.

Turn right onto Saint Johnland Road, where you will shortly pass the Obediah Smith House on the right. Constructed in 1700, it was the home of a grandson of the town's founder and is now preserved by the town's historical society. (If you wish to return to Smithtown, turn left onto Saint Johnland. Continue straight onto Route 25A, then follow it east into Smithtown.)

Continue to the first traffic light; then turn right onto Old Dock Road. At its end lies **Kings Park Bluff**, a favorite haven for weekend mariners. Across the bay you can spot Short Beach and, in the distance, the Connecticut shore. For lunch, the Old Dock Inn offers elegant seafood dining.

Return to Saint Johnland and turn right. Now called Sunken Meadow Road, the route takes on a roller-coaster–like profile with many ups and downs. Just before the road crosses under a stone bridge, dismount and enter **Sunken Meadow State Park** through the

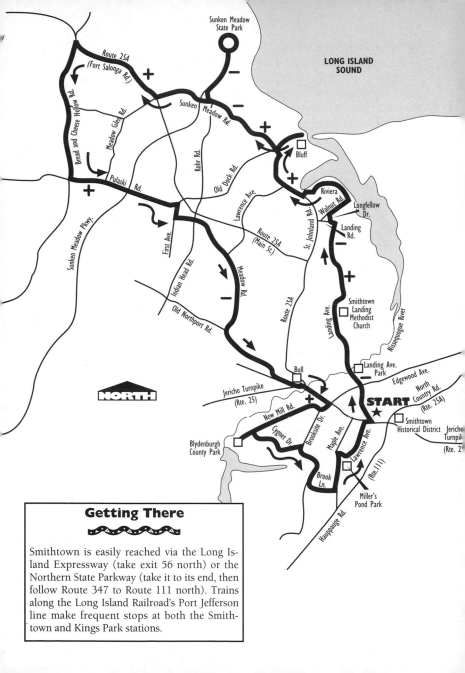

Sunken Meadow
State Park

LONG ISLAND
SOUND

Route 25A
(Fort Salonga Rd.)

Bread and Cheese Hollow Rd.

Meadow Glen Rd.

Sunken Meadow Rd.

Kohr Rd.

Old Dock Rd.

Pulaski Rd.

Sunken Meadow Pkwy.

First Ave.

Indian Head Rd.

Old Northport Rd.

Meadow Rd.

Lawrence Ave.

Route 25A
(Main St.)

St. Johnland Rd.

Bluff

Riviera

Walnut Rd.

Longfellow
Dr.

Landing
Rd.

Route 25A

Landing Ave.

Smithtown
Landing
Methodist
Church

Nissequogue River

Bull

Landing Ave.
Park

Edgewood Ave.

North
Country Rd.
(Rte. 25A)

Jericho Turnpike
(Rte. 25)

New Mill Rd.

Cygnet Dr.

Brookside Dr.

Maple Ave.

Lawrence Ave.

START

Smithtown
Historical District

Jericho
Turnpik
(Rte. 2

Blydenburgh
County Park

Brook
Ln.

(Rte. 111)

Miller's
Pond Park

Hauppauge Rd.

NORTH

Getting There

Smithtown is easily reached via the Long Island Expressway (take exit 56 north) or the
Northern State Parkway (take it to its end, then
follow Route 347 to Route 111 north). Trains
along the Long Island Railroad's Port Jefferson
line make frequent stops at both the Smithtown and Kings Park stations.

DIREC-TIONS at a glance

0.0	From town center head north on Landing Avenue.
2.9	Left onto Landing Road.
3.0	Right onto Longfellow Drive.
3.1	Right onto Walnut Road.
3.4	Left onto Riviera Drive.
4.0	At fork, keep right on Riviera.
4.3	Right onto Saint Johnland Road.
5.2	Right onto Old Dock Road, continuing to its end. Turn around, returning to the Saint Johnland/Sunken Meadow Road intersection. Right onto Sunken Meadow Road.
7.3	Right through gate into Sunken Meadow Park.
8.3	Exit park back through gate. Continue right (west) on Sunken Meadow Road.
9.0	Right onto Fort Salonga Road (Route 25A).
10.8	Left onto Bread and Cheese Hollow Road.
12.9	Left onto Pulaski Road.
14.4	Right onto First Avenue.
14.6	Left onto Meadow Road.
16.6	Left at flashing light to continue on Meadow Road.
17.6	Left at traffic light to stay on Meadow Road.
18.0	Left onto Jericho Turnpike (Route 25).
18.5	Right onto Brooksite Drive.
18.7	Right onto New Mill Road.
19.9	Straight into Blydenburgh Park. Exit through same gate back onto New Mill Road.
20.2	Right onto Cygnet Drive.
21.0	Right onto Brooksite Drive.
21.6	Left onto Brook Lane.
22.1	Left onto Maple Avenue.
22.6	Right onto Lawrence Avenue.
23.3	Right onto Route 25.

pedestrian gate on the right. Located on Long Island Sound, the park is best known for its mile-long beach and boardwalk. Also found within its 1,266 acres are numerous picnic areas, playgrounds, and hiking trails. After you have explored the park, exit as you entered and continue down Sunken Meadow Road to Fort Salonga Road (Route 25A). (For a hilly shortcut, continue straight and follow Meadow Glen Road to Pulaski Road, then turn left.)

As you approach the Fort Salonga Shopping Center (where there are restaurants, a deli, and a supermarket), turn left onto Bread and Cheese Hollow Road. A flat run, Bread and Cheese Hollow winds along the Smithtown-Huntington town line, wedged between two ridges. At its end take a left onto Pulaski Road for an uphill battle into the Kings Park section of Smithtown.

Exit Kings Park on Meadow Road, a (mostly) downhill trek that leads all the way to Jericho Turnpike (Route 25). After turning left to join Jericho and passing under the Long Island Railroad trestle, watch out for the **bull** on the left. A **bull?** That's right, but it's not a real bull; rather it's a statue commemorating Smithtown's founding in 1665. According to legend, local Indians agreed to sell Richard Smythe, the town's founder, as much land as he could circle in one day while riding a bull. Smythe supposedly set out on his bull Whisper on the day of the summer solstice, completing a 35-mile journey by nightfall. Historians debate the accuracy of this tale, but the statue of Whisper has nevertheless become a county landmark.

Stay on Jericho to the top of the next hill; then take a quick right onto Brookside Drive and another onto New Mill Road. New Mill, which passes through a serene neighborhood of homes, offers one of the nicest cycling environments on the entire ride. Follow it all the way to its end to enter **Blydenburgh County Park.** Inside, many hiking trails, playgrounds, and picnic areas surround Stump Pond, a beautiful body of water. The pond was created at the turn of the century when residents dammed the Nissequogue River using tree stumps (hence the name). Rental boats are available, as are a limited number of campsites. If you have never tried bicycle camping before, here is the perfect chance. Pack as lightly as possible (hiking gear is a must) and enjoy!

The ride concludes by zigzagging through other tranquil residential neighborhoods. You may want to make a last stop at **Miller's Pond Park**, located on Maple Avenue. The pond is usually swarming with ducks, geese, and swans, all eagerly vying for the bread thrown by visitors. From the park take a right onto Lawrence Avenue for the final sprint back into the town center.

For Further Information

Smithtown Historical Society (516) 265–6768
Sunken Meadow State Park (516) 269–4333
Blydenburgh County Park (516) 360–4966

Westchester County, New York

Harrison to Rye

Mileage:	16
Terrain:	Hilly in spots
Traffic:	Light to moderate
Facilities:	Water fountains and rest rooms in the Harrison Town Library, Rye Nature Center, Playland, and Rye Town Park; Delis in the center of Harrison, as well as near the ride's starting point along Milton Road
Things to see:	Station Park, Haviland Family Cemetery, Westchester Country Club, Rye Nature Center, Rye Beach and Playland

Though the two towns coexist peacefully today, the early ties between Harrison and Rye were anything but tranquil. The trouble started in 1662, when four settlers purchased much of the area from the Siwanoy Indians. Unfortunately, the settlers failed to apply for a patent; as a result, their claim was never officially sanctioned by the provincial government. In 1695 part of the same land was sold to John Harrison, who had the land surveyed by the British government and was subsequently granted a patent. With tempers flaring over this series of events, Rye temporarily seceded from New York. Though the wounds soon healed, the distinction between the towns remained vague until 1788, when the county finally recognized Harrison as a separate township.

Begin your tour of the towns at **Station Park**, adjacent to the Harrison Railroad Station at the corner of Heineman Place and Harrison

Avenue (Route 127). Begin by heading north on Harrison Avenue. In about a mile turn left onto Sterling Road, followed by another left at the fork onto Woodlands Road. Both take you through a lovely neighborhood of attractive homes. Stay to the left at each of the stop signs that you will meet along the way.

Woodlands Road ends at Pleasant Ridge Road, where the ride turns right. Not too far down on the left side of Pleasant Ridge, watch for a small cemetery set back from the road. This is the **Haviland Family Cemetery**, and it contains several dozen headstones dating back to the early 1800s.

Continue straight across the intersection with North Street (Route 127) onto Polly Park Road. Polly Park is a challenging road, not so much for the hills (though there are a few) as for its rutted surface. Be careful.

Just before Polly Park meets Purchase Street, turn right onto Belmont Avenue and enter the posh world of the **Westchester Country Club**. Circle around the club's immaculate grounds by taking Belmont around to the left, followed by a right onto Park Drive. Originally known as the Westchester Biltmore, the country club opened in 1922 on the site of the former Hobart Park Farm. Designed by John Bowman, the club became an instant world-class showpiece thanks to its huge clubhouse, three golf courses, polo field, and tennis and squash courts. Half a century later it remains one of the premier examples of opulent living and is perhaps best known as the site of the annual Westchester Open professional golf tournament. The regal flavor continues to the end of Park Drive as you pedal past some truly elegant homes set on immaculately manicured lawns.

Turn left and head south on North Street (Route 127). After passing St. Vincent's Hospital, turn left at the traffic light to continue along North Street. (For a quick return to the starting point, follow Route 127 south to Station Park.) Soon you will pass the Willow Ridge Golf Club on the left and Greenwood Union Cemetery on the right. Coasting past the cemetery, you will cross the town line of Harrison and enter neighboring Rye.

After riding up and over the railroad tracks and the New England Thruway (Interstate 95), turn left onto Theodore Fremd Avenue. This

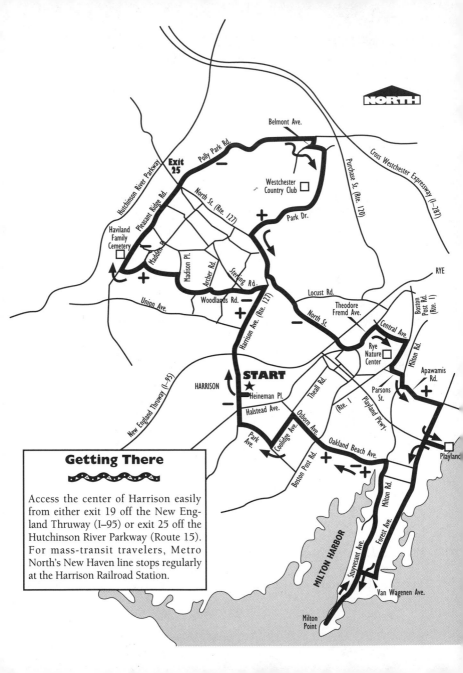

NORTH

Belmont Ave.

Polly Park Rd.

Exit 25

Hutchinson River Parkway

Pleasant Ridge Rd.

North St. (Rte. 127)

Westchester Country Club

Purchase St. (Rte. 120)

Cross Westchester Expressway (I–287)

Park Dr.

Haviland Family Cemetery

Madden Rd.

Madison Pl.

Archer Rd.

Sterling Rd.

RYE

Boston Post Rd. (Rte. 1)

Union Ave.

Woodlands Rd.

Locust Rd.

Theodore Fremd Ave.

Central Ave.

Milton Rd.

Harrison Ave. (Rte. 127)

North St.

Rye Nature Center

Apawamis Rd.

New England Thruway (I–95)

HARRISON

START

Heineman Pl.

Theall Rd.

Parsons St.

Playland Pkwy.

Halstead Ave.

Osborn Ave.

(Rte. 1)

Park Ave.

Coolidge Ave.

Oakland Beach Ave.

Boston Post Rd.

Milton Rd.

Playland

Getting There

Access the center of Harrison easily from either exit 19 off the New England Thruway (I–95) or exit 25 off the Hutchinson River Parkway (Route 15). For mass-transit travelers, Metro North's New Haven line stops regularly at the Harrison Railroad Station.

MILTON HARBOR

Stuyvesant Ave.

Forest Ave.

Milton Rd.

Van Wagenen Ave.

Milton Point

DIREC-TIONS
at a glance

0.0	Begin at Station Park at the corner of Harrison Avenue (Route 127) and Heineman Place. North on Harrison.
1.1	Left onto Sterling Road.
1.2	Left onto Woodlands Road.
2.0	Left at stop sign to stay on Woodlands Road.
2.3	Left again at stop sign to stay on Woodlands Road.
2.6	Right onto Pleasant Ridge Road.
3.5	Straight across North Street (Route 127) onto Polly Park Road.
5.0	Right onto Belmont Avenue.
5.1	Left to stay on Belmont Avenue.
5.2	Right onto Park Drive.
6.5	Left onto North Street (Route 127).
7.0	Left at traffic light to stay on North Street.
8.0	Left onto Theodore Fremd Avenue.
8.4	Right onto Central Avenue.
8.7	Right onto Boston Post Road (Route 1).
9.0	Left onto Parsons Street.
9.2	Right onto Milton Road.
9.3	Left onto Apawamis Road.
9.7	Right onto Forest Avenue.
11.3	Right onto Van Wagenen Avenue.
11.5	Left onto Stuyvesant Avenue.
12.0	Turn around at end of Stuyvesant Avenue.
13.1	Right onto Milton Road.
13.5	Left onto Oakland Beach Avenue.
14.5	Left onto Coolidge Avenue.
14.9	Right onto Park Avenue.
15.1	Right onto Harrison Avenue (Route 127).
15.6	Back at Station Park.

is followed by a right in 0.4 mile onto Central Avenue. Another right at its end puts you on the Boston Post Road (Route 1) westbound.

For the next 0.25 mile, the road parallels a small woodland strip on the right. Within, an unpaved footpath follows Blind Brook as both approach the main entrance to **Rye Nature Center.** Turn into the center's entrance road and continue up and along to the visitors' center.

The nature center is located on the grounds of the former estate of financier Marselis Parsons. In 1906 Parsons built a huge mansion that must surely have been the talk of the town. Then came the Stock Market crash of 1929, and Parsons lost most of his fortune. Adding to the family's losses was a fire of "mysterious origin" that leveled the mansion in 1942. All that remains of this grand home is its massive stone foundation with two chimneys towering above. Three years after the fire, the town of Rye purchased thirty-five acres of the estate; an additional twelve were acquired between 1959 and 1964.

Today the Rye Nature Center features a museum, a solar greenhouse, a research laboratory, and more than 2.5 miles of hiking trails. These trails meander through open fields and dense forests and past pond and stream environments. A self-guided interpretive tour helps visitors learn about the more than 70 different species of trees, 125 types of wildflowers, and more than 180 species of birds that inhabit the woods. The center is open daily, though the museum is closed on Sunday. There is no charge for admission.

Exiting the center, turn left onto Parsons Street, followed by a right onto Milton Road, a left onto Apawamis Road, and finally a right onto Forest Avenue. In 0.25 mile you will pass an intersection with Playland Parkway, where a left will take you to **Rye Beach** and **Playland Amusement Park.** When it opened in 1928, Playland was one of the nation's first planned amusement parks. Since then it has grown to include more than fifty rides, a horseshoe-shaped beach and boardwalk, and a large saltwater lake. Playland is noted among amusement-park connoisseurs for its wooden "Dragon Coaster" and vintage merry-go-round, while students of architecture enjoy the art deco buildings found along the grassy central mall. Though there is no admission charge into the park itself, tickets are required for the amusements. Park hours vary by season, so it's best to call before you visit.

Proceed to the end of Forest. Turn right onto Van Wagenen Avenue and left onto Stuyvesant Avenue. Stuyvesant continues past several ritzy yacht clubs on its way toward the tip of Milton Point.

When you can't go any farther, turn around to begin the journey back home. Follow Stuyvesant to Milton Road; then turn left onto Oakland Beach Avenue. After crossing Boston Post Road (Route 1), the road changes names to Osborn Avenue. As Osborn heads downhill, turn left onto Coolidge Avenue. Two right turns, one onto Park Avenue and another onto Harrison Avenue (Route 127), bring you back into the center of Harrison. One final climb over the railroad tracks returns you to Station Park.

For Further Information

Westchester Country Club (914) 967–6000
Rye Nature Center (914) 967–5150
Playland (914) 967–2040

Westchester County, New York

Kensico Reservoir Loop

Mileage:	15
Terrain:	Hilly
Traffic:	Light
Facilities:	Rest rooms and water at ride's starting point in Kensico Dam Plaza and at Cranberry Lake Preserve; a deli and diner in Valhalla, on Broadway just beyond the turn-off onto North Kensico Avenue; water, rest rooms, and food at Westchester County Airport
Things to see:	Kensico Reservoir, Kensico Dam Plaza, Cranberry Lake Preserve

Of the many reservoirs and lakes scattered throughout upper Westchester County, none is more beautiful than **Kensico Reservoir.** The reservoir is situated in a long, slender valley surrounded by hills on three sides and Kensico Dam on the fourth. The dam began as an earthen embankment in 1885. It was subsequently enlarged to its present size by 1917, to provide more drinking water to a thirsty New York City.

Begin your circuit of Kensico Reservoir from the park at the base of Kensico Dam. **Kensico Dam Plaza** features many paved trails around the base of the dam, providing hours of fascination for nature lovers. In addition, the plaza, maintained by the Westchester County Department of Parks, hosts outdoor concerts and other activities during the warmer months.

Take a right turn out of Kensico Plaza onto Broadway in Valhalla and get ready to scale the height of the dam as you turn right onto North Kensico Avenue. The road travels, in effect, from the base of the dam to the shore of the reservoir in only 0.2 mile. Its rutted concrete surface only adds to the difficulty of the climb; most readers probably will do best by dismounting their bikes and walking its length.

Once at the end of North Kensico Avenue, turn left onto West Lake Drive and enjoy the view! Kensico Reservoir covers 13.3 square miles and holds more than 30 billion gallons of water. Direct public access to its shore is strictly limited in an effort to minimize possible pollution.

West Lake Drive ends at the intersection with Columbus Avenue. Or does it? Take a right onto Columbus, followed by another right just down the road back onto West Lake Drive. After passing a reservoir maintenance complex, West Lake Drive takes on a wooded, rural personality and is free of heavy traffic. Though it has its ups and downs, you will enjoy the scenic ride. All along, watch as the reservoir peeks through the trees on the right. An especially lovely view is found as the road bends sharply to the right around a deep crevice in the land.

Civilization returns as West Lake Drive begins to ascend. Follow the accompanying map carefully, zigging to the left and zagging to the right as indicated. As the road straightens out, enjoy a long, slow downhill coast toward the campus of West Lake High School and the village of Thornwood.

Stay on West Lake Drive as it veers around a monstrous green water tank and continues all the way to its end at Nanny Hagen Road. A right at this juncture takes you back toward Kensico Reservoir and its enclosing wilderness. In about a mile the road takes a sharp right. Off to the right the view of the water is truly outstanding; just be careful around that curve—it's a long way down!

Nanny Hagen Road continues to play hide-and-seek with the reservoir until it ends at King Street (Route 120). Though busier than Nanny Hagen Road, King Street is a pleasant highway for cycling, thanks to a broad, smooth shoulder. (The only point of concern should be where Route 22 joins in from the left; the traffic there can be a bit harrowing.)

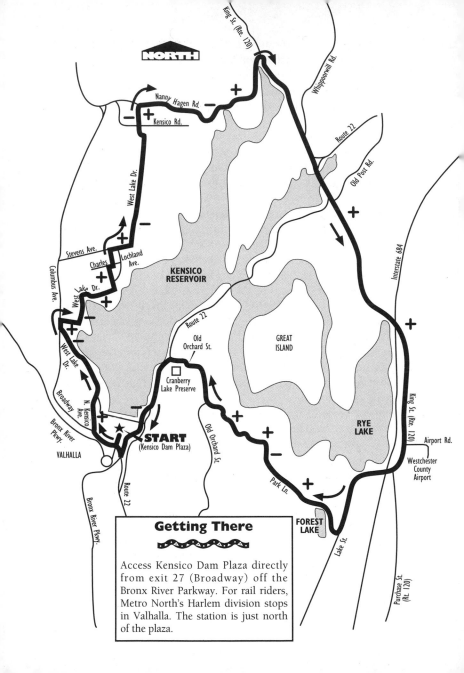

NORTH

King St. (Rte. 120)

Whippoorwill Rd.

Nanny Hagen Rd.

Kensico Rd.

Route 22

Old Post Rd.

West Lake Dr.

Interstate 684

Stevens Ave.

Charles

Lochland Ave.

KENSICO RESERVOIR

West Lake Dr.

Columbus Ave.

Route 22

GREAT ISLAND

Old Orchard St.

Cranberry Lake Preserve

West Lake Dr.

RYE LAKE

Broadway

N. Kensico Ave.

King St. (Rte. 120)

Airport Rd.

★ START
(Kensico Dam Plaza)

Westchester County Airport

Bronx River Pkwy.

VALHALLA

Old Orchard St.

Park Ln.

Route 22

Bronx River Pkwy.

Lake St.

FOREST LAKE

Purchase St. (Rte. 120)

Getting There

Access Kensico Dam Plaza directly from exit 27 (Broadway) off the Bronx River Parkway. For rail riders, Metro North's Harlem division stops in Valhalla. The station is just north of the plaza.

0.0	Leave Kensico Dam Plaza and turn right onto Broadway.
0.5	Right onto North Kensico Avenue.
0.7	Left onto West Lake Drive.
1.6	Right onto Columbus Avenue.
1.7	Right onto West Lake Drive.
2.5	Left to follow West Lake Drive.
2.7	Right to stay on West Lake Drive (Charles Street enters on left).
2.8	Left to follow West Lake Drive (Lochland Avenue continues straight).
2.9	Right to stay on West Lake Drive (Stevens Avenue enters on left).
4.5	Right onto Nanny Hagen Road.
6.1	Right onto King Street (Route 120).
7.6	Left at traffic light to follow Route 120.
10.3	As Route 120 turns left, continue straight on Lake Street.
11.0	Right onto Park Lane.
12.7	Continue diagonally right onto Old Orchard Street.
13.4	Left onto Route 22.
14.1	Right toward Bronx River and Taconic Parkways.
14.7	Right at stop sign onto Broadway.
14.8	Straight into Kensico Plaza.

Continue to the left on Route 120 South as Route 22 peels off to the right. (If you want to return to Kensico Plaza more quickly, stay on Route 22, which meets up with the ride at Old Orchard Street in 1.8 miles. But be forewarned: The route is both hilly and narrow in spots.) Though it begins with a narrow, uphill run itself, Route 120 quickly opens up and flattens out as it nears the New York–Connecticut state line. A bit farther along it wedges between Westchester County Airport, on the other side of the hills to the left, and an extension of Kensico Reservoir known as Rye Lake on the right.

As Route 120 turns left, the route continues straight on Lake Street. After crossing over Interstate 684 a second time, take the next right onto Park Lane. Although the road sign is easy to miss, you should have no trouble spotting the sign for the Hillside Farm Nursery. After joining Park the route meanders past Forest Lake, a small body of water surrounded by unspoiled woodlands. Park is a bit on the narrow and windy side, but the light traffic makes it an acceptable challenge for cycling.

Park ends at a stop sign, with your route jogging to the right onto Old Orchard Street. Bordering the road to the left is **Cranberry Lake Preserve.** It was from here that the stones for Kensico Dam were exhumed and transported by a special rail line in 1915. Today Cranberry Preserve contains miles of hiking trails for nature lovers to enjoy. Bicycles may be locked near the park's ranger station.

About 0.7 mile after joining Route 22 for your final sprint back to Kensico Plaza, be on the lookout for a sign pointing toward the Bronx River and Taconic Parkways. Take that road as it plunges off of Route 22 and down toward Broadway. (You will know you missed this turnoff if you come to the intersection with West Lake Drive; carefully turn around and try again.) At the bottom of the hill, turn right onto Broadway and continue straight back into Kensico Dam Plaza.

The Bronx River Parkway is closed to automobiles from 10:00 A.M. to 2:00 P.M. every Sunday from May through September (except holiday weekends) for "Bicycle Sunday." Cyclists can ride worry-free on these days from the County Center in White Plains to Scarsdale Road in Yonkers, a 14-mile round trip.

For Further Information

Bicycle Sunday (914) 285–PARK
Cranberry Lake Preserve (914) 428–1005

Westchester County, New York
Bedford and Vicinity

Mileage:	17
Terrain:	Hilly, with some dirt roads
Traffic:	Light
Facilities:	Food store for last-minute supplies in the center of Bedford; water and rest rooms at the Mianus River Gorge
Things to see:	Bedford Historic Village Green, Sutton Clock Tower, Byram Lake, Middle Patent Rural Cemetery, Mianus River Gorge Wildlife Refuge

Located in the picturesque surroundings of mid-Westchester County, Bedford represents the quintessential small town. The village is built around the large, tree-lined **Bedford Historic Village Green** and comprises a number of small stores (including a highly recommended delicatessen) and historical buildings that you may want to visit.

The town green is a favorite starting point among local cyclists for many adventures. This ride passes several historic and natural landmarks, while covering a wide variety of local roads. Before embarking, note that you will pass over several short stretches of dirt road. While quite well maintained by the highway department, they require extra care on the part of the rider.

From the village center head north for a short distance on Cantitoe Road (Route 22). Just over a rise beyond town, as Cantitoe Road veers to the right, take a left-hand turn onto Guard Hill Road. Guard Hill Road is rich in colonial history, as it was one of the first routes cleared by early area settlers.

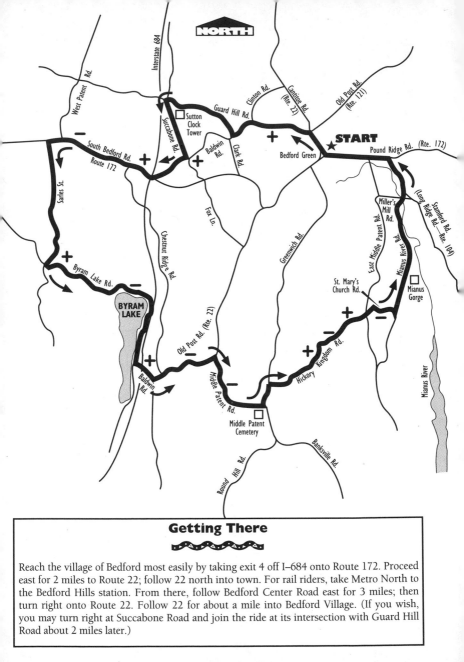

Getting There

Reach the village of Bedford most easily by taking exit 4 off I–684 onto Route 172. Proceed east for 2 miles to Route 22; follow 22 north into town. For rail riders, take Metro North to the Bedford Hills station. From there, follow Bedford Center Road east for 3 miles; then turn right onto Route 22. Follow 22 for about a mile into Bedford Village. (If you wish, you may turn right at Succabone Road and join the ride at its intersection with Guard Hill Road about 2 miles later.)

DIREC-TIONS at a glance

0.0	Head north on Cantitoe Road (Route 22).
0.3	Left onto Guard Hill Road.
2.4	Left onto Succabone Road.
3.1	Right onto Baldwin Road.
3.7	Right onto South Bedford Road (Route 172).
5.5	Left onto Sarles Street.
7.0	Left onto Byram Lake Road.
9.4	Left onto unmarked Baldwin Road.
9.8	Left onto Old Post Road (Route 22).
10.6	Right onto Middle Patent Road.
11.6	Left onto Greenwich Road.
12.0	Right onto Hickory Kingdom Road.
13.8	At Saint Mary's Church, continue straight onto Saint Mary's Church Road.
14.3	Left onto Mianus River Road.
15.8	Right onto Miller's Mill Road, then left after crossing river.
15.9	Left onto Stamford Road (Route 104).
16.5	Left onto Pound Ridge Road (Route 172).
17.3	At the village green, bear right back into Bedford.

As you approach the intersection with Clinton Road, Guard Hill begins to alternate between a paved and dirt surface. Though actually smoother than some paved roads in the area, the dirt sections should be navigated slowly, especially after a recent rain. Fortunately, most of the uphill portions are paved.

At the intersection of Guard Hill and Succabone Roads is a famous local landmark, the **Sutton Clock Tower.** Erected in 1939, the tower houses a fine, century-old clock complete with a 550-pound bell. The clock was originally installed in the barn of local residents Mr. and Mrs. James Sutton. Although the barn burned in 1929, the clock and bell were saved and, a decade later, were installed in the current tower after a group of Bedford citizens raised funds for its construction. The clock continues to be maintained by the Bedford Historical Society and is wound weekly by its neighbors.

At the clock, turn left onto Succabone Road. For the next few miles, as you go from Succabone to Baldwin Road and South Bedford Road (Route 172), you are faced with a mostly uphill run. The pain of the hills is tempered somewhat by their scenic beauty, thanks to some woods, fields, and an occasional barn. You finally reach the hill's summit about a mile after joining South Bedford Road, only to head quickly back down. Take care not to build up too much speed, as it is easy to flash past your next left-hand turn onto Sarles Street.

Follow Sarles for about 1.5 miles to a four-way intersection with Byram Lake Road, where the route again turns left. Approaching the lake itself, the road slopes steeply downward and is especially narrow and curvy. With the pavement giving way to a hard dirt surface, the route travels along the north and east shores of **Byram Lake**. The lake is outstanding for its natural beauty, especially in the autumn, and makes an ideal midway stopping point for an impromptu roadside picnic.

Your next turn, onto Baldwin Road, is unmarked but easily identifiable as an uphill run passing under Interstate 684 and ending at Old Post Road (Route 22). At the intersection with Old Post Road, begin a long and refreshing downhill trek that glides all the way to the end of Middle Patent Road, where you will find the **Middle Patent Rural Cemetery** on the corner of Middle Patent and Greenwich Roads. Established in 1743, this colonial cemetery holds the graves of fifteen Revolutionary War soldiers. Just beyond the opposite corner is the Middle Patent Methodist/Episcopal Church, built in 1825.

The ride continues to the left on Greenwich Road for a short distance, then right onto Hickory Kingdom Road. The latter crosses some of the hilliest terrain on the entire route and may well require riders to dismount and walk a bit. (To shorten the ride, follow Greenwich Road all the way to its end, then turn right onto Route 22 back into Bedford.)

Continue as straight as possible through the confusing intersection with East Middle Patent Road. The journey curves around and behind Saint Mary's Episcopal Church (built in 1851), zigzagging down a steep hill and onto narrow Saint Mary's Church Road.

Turning left onto Mianus River Road, you again travel along a serene, little-used thoroughfare. About halfway down the road lies the **Mianus River Gorge Wildlife Refuge.** For those who have a little extra energy, many enjoyable hours may be spent exploring this unique, untouched haven. Beginning at the small visitors' shelter, three footpaths of varying lengths (1, 2, and 5 miles) allow hikers to explore the flora and fauna of this beautiful gorge. We personally recommend taking the longer "C" trail, which takes explorers past 300-year-old hemlocks, an eighteenth-century mica quarry, and picturesque Havemeyer Falls.

As Mianus River Road continues, the pavement once again alternates between finished and unfinished surfaces. Bearing right at the road's end onto Miller's Mill Road, continue over the small bridge and then turn left past Miller's Mill itself. Follow Stamford Road (Route 104) north, then Pound Ridge Road (Route 172) west into Bedford and the village green starting point.

For Further Information

Bedford Historical Society (914) 234–9328
Mianus River Gorge Wildlife Refuge (914) 234–3455

Westchester County, New York

Katonah and Croton Reservoir

Mileage:	33
Terrain:	Hilly
Traffic:	Light
Facilities:	Ample selection of supplies for the ride at the Katonah Deli, at the ride's starting point; water and rest room facilities at Muscoot Farm, Croton Gorge Park and Teatown Lake Reservation
Things to see:	Croton Reservoir, Muscoot Farm, Croton Gorge Park, Teatown Lake Reservation, Elephant Hotel (optional)

A century ago the town of Katonah was much different[2]—and much drier—than it is today. In 1894 town officials were informed of a decision made by the New York City Board of Water Supply to flood most of Katonah's lowlands to create a vast reservoir. Facing a crisis that would change the village for all generations to come, the town board voted to move most of the affected homes to new, higher plots of land. This meant lifting each structure off its foundation, towing it by horses over timber tracks to a new site, and then securing it to a new substructure.

A second project authorized by the town board created a new, grand village center. Bedford Road was widened to 100 feet across. Opposing one-way wagon paths were separated by a grassy strip planted with trees and flowers. Although the wagon paths have since been paved for modern horseless carriages, Bedford Road (now Route

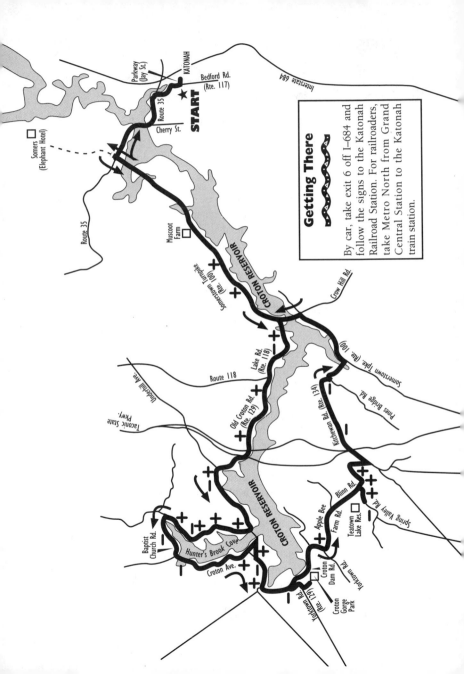

START

KATONAH

Parkway (Jay St.)

Bedford Rd. (Rte. 117)

Interstate 684

Route 35

Cherry St.

Somers (Elephant Hotel)

Route 35

Muscoot Farm

Somerstown Turnpike (Rte. 100)

CROTON RESERVOIR

Crow Hill Rd.

Lake Rd. (Rte. 118)

Route 118

Somerstown Tpke. (Rte. 100)

Pines Bridge Rd.

Linden Ave.

Taconic State Pkwy.

Old Croton Rd. (Rte. 129)

Kitchewan Rd. (Rte. 134)

CROTON RESERVOIR

Baptist Church Rd.

Hunter's Brook Cove

Croton Ave.

Apple Bee Farm Rd.

Blinn Rd.

Teatown Lake Res.

Spring Valley Rd.

Croton Dam Rd.

Yorktown Rd.

Yorktown Rd. (Rte. 129)

Croton Gorge Park

Getting There

By car, take exit 6 off I-684 and follow the signs to the Katonah Railroad Station. For railroaders, take Metro North from Grand Central Station to the Katonah train station.

	0.0	Right at the corner of the Parkway and Bedford Road (Route 117).
	0.5	Left onto Route 35 west.
	1.9	Left onto Somerstown Turnpike (Route 100 south).
	6.4	Right onto Lake Road (Route 118 north).

7.6 Straight to join Old Croton Road (Route 129 west).

11.2 Right onto Hunterbrook Road.

13.1 Left onto Baptist Church Road.

13.9 Left onto Croton Avenue.

15.5 Right onto Yorktown Road (Route 129 west).

17.1 Left into Croton Gorge Park. When exiting the park, turn right and continue back the way you came.

18.0 Right onto Croton Dam Road.

18.9 Right onto Yorktown Road.

19.3 Left onto Apple Bee Farm Road (later changes name to Blinn Road).

20.5 Right onto Spring Valley Road.

20.9 Right into Teatown Lake Reservation. When exiting, return to the Spring Valley–Blinn intersection.

21.3 Right to continue on Spring Valley Road.

21.9 Left onto Kitchewan Road (Route 134 east).

24.4 Left onto Somerstown Turnpike (Route 100 north).

25.9 Left over bridge across reservoir.

26.2 Continue straight on Route 100 north.

30.7 Right at intersection with Route 35 (or continue straight ahead 4 miles into Somers).

32.6 Back into Katonah.

117) retains its century-old charm.

Lining the road are many charming buildings from that long-ago era. One of the finest is the Methodist-Episcopal Church, which features cobblestoned floors and an open belfry. For art lovers the Katonah Gallery, located at the rear of the Katonah Public Library, has frequently changing exhibits. Another spot worth a visit is the Katonah Deli across the road—a great place to fuel up for the ride ahead!

On this trip you will tour the reservoir that almost sunk the town. **Croton Reservoir** is a scenic body of water that provides a great backdrop for cycling. Begin at the corner of Jay Street (known officially as the Parkway at this point) and Bedford Road, heading north out of town on the latter. Bear left at the end of Bedford onto Route 35. In about a mile you will catch your first view of the water.

Entering the town of Somers, watch for the sign proclaiming this as the BIRTHPLACE OF THE AMERICAN CIRCUS (more about this later). At the junction with Somerstown Turnpike (Route 100), turn left and begin the journey along the reservoir's north shore. This road is one of the county's best for cycling, thanks to its wide shoulder—and the view isn't bad either!

One mile later, keep an eye out for a sign on the right leading into **Muscoot Farm.** The farm was owned by the Hopkins family for three generations. It was sold to Westchester County in 1968 and subsequently enlarged to its present 777 acres. Not just a museum to the past, the farm is a true working agricultural complex. During any given visit you might find cows being milked, sheep being shorn, or fields being sown, weeded, or harvested. The main house was built in the 1880s and relocated to its present site in 1894, the year of the flood. It is currently used for cooking demonstrations, classes, and art exhibits. Trails extend throughout the farm; the longest (the "yellow" trail) can be hiked in about two hours.

Route 100 crosses Croton Reservoir on its way toward Millwood but the ride continues to the right on Lake Road (Route 118). After 1 mile Route 118 takes a right but you should continue straight on Old Croton Road (Route 129). You will immediately notice two things about Routes 118 and 129: they are both much narrower and much hillier than Route 100. But the striking scenery will make the aches worth it.

Just before Route 129 crosses over the reservoir on Hunter Bridge, turn right onto Hunterbrook Road. Once again the hills come on strong as the road winds northward along a small inlet off the reservoir. In about 2 miles a quick left turn at a four-way intersection brings you onto Baptist Church Road. Another left onto Croton Avenue takes you southward along the opposite bank of Hunters Brook Cove. At the road's end, rejoin Route 129 and continue westward. (If your legs are not up to the hills of Hunterbrook Road, continue straight across the bridge instead.)

After passing the left turn onto Croton Dam Road, take the next left off Route 129 into **Croton Gorge Park**. (The entrance is midway down a steep hill.) The park, surrounding the base of Croton Dam, offers an unparalleled view of the reservoir's overflow waters crashing through the dam's gates and over manmade waterfalls. Footpaths take hikers through the park, while a shaded picnic area makes a pleasant midride resting spot.

Back on the bike, return to Route 129 and turn right onto Croton Dam Road (whew, what a hill!), crossing the dam itself. Continue to the road's end; then bear right for a short stint on Yorktown Road. At the next left, turn onto Apple Bee Farm Road and begin another climb. You will pass the farm itself toward the hill's peak. A little farther along, the road's name changes to Blinn Road. Regardless of the label, the trip is curvy and bumpy and must be ridden cautiously.

Blinn soon ends at Spring Valley Road. Turning right onto Spring Valley, you will come to **Teatown Lake Reservation** over the first hill. The reservation began development in 1963 after the county was given 190 acres by the Gerard Swope family. Centrally located in the reservation is a beautiful thirty-three-acre lake surrounded by marshland, forest, and meadows. Hiking trails lead away from the visitors' center and pass throughout the property. One path, called the "Back 40" trail, offers a spectacular 10-mile view of the lower Hudson Valley. Many visitors come to enjoy the colorful wildflowers or the many songbirds that call Teatown home, while others simply come to enjoy the silence and serenity.

Return to the Spring Valley–Blinn intersection for the half-mile trek to Kitchewan Road (Route 134). From Kitchewan take a left onto Somerstown Turnpike (Route 100 north) and proceed across Croton Reservoir for the trip home.

If you have a little extra energy, rather than heading immediately back to Katonah, continue north into the center of Somers (about 4 miles farther up Route 100). As the sign proclaimed earlier, Somers is the birthplace of the American circus. The story begins in 1825, when Hachaliah Bailey built a hotel in the center of town. He named the building the **Elephant Hotel** to commemorate Old Bet, an African elephant he had purchased ten years earlier. Bailey created a "rolling menagerie" of animals that traveled across the countryside. Thus, the traveling circus was born.

Today the Elephant Hotel acts as the Somers Town Hall as well as the home of the Somers Historical Society. Inside, a small museum tracing the history of the circus is open on Friday afternoon and Saturday morning. Admission is free. Across the street a small statue immortalizes Old Bet for all to see.

For Further Information

Katonah Gallery (914) 232–4988
Muscoot Farm (914) 232–7118
Croton Gorge Park (914) 271–3293
Teatown Lake Reservation (914) 762–2912
Elephant Hotel (914) 277–4977

Westchester County, New York

Titicus Reservoir Quickie

Mileage:	12 (24 with optional side trip)
Terrain:	Rolling
Traffic:	Mostly light
Facilities:	Deli at the intersection of Routes 22 and 116, the ride's starting point, for any last-minute food supplies you might need for the ride; water and rest rooms in the Hammond Museum as well as at Ward Pound Ridge Reservation
Things to see:	Titicus Reservoir, North Salem Historic District, Hammond Museum, Balanced Rock, Ward Pound Ridge Reservation (optional), Mill's Road Cemetery

Cycling the roads of upper Westchester can be both an exhausting and an exhilarating experience. Many long, high hills test a cyclist's conditioning and endurance. Here is a short ride that offers a little relief from all that, while still including a few challenging climbs.

Begin in Purdys at the intersection of Routes 22 and 116, which is directly accessible from exit 7 off Interstate 684. There is ample parking along the roadside for those who must drive to the departure point, as well as a deli in case you want to stock up on provisions before leaving.

Head north on Routes 22/116, turning to the right just ahead as Route 116 (Titicus Road) veers to the east. **Titicus Reservoir** will

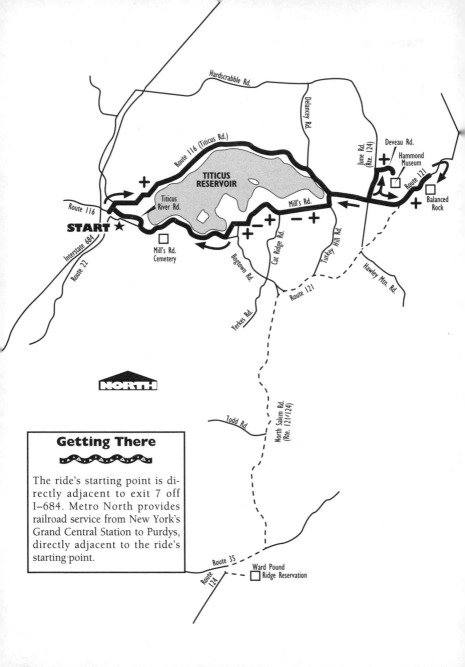

Hardscrabble Rd.

Delancey Rd.

June Rd. (Rte. 124)

Deveau Rd.

Hammond Museum

Route 121

Route 116 (Titicus Rd.)

TITICUS RESERVOIR

Balanced Rock

Route 116

Titicus River Rd.

Mill's Rd.

START ★

Interstate 684

Route 22

Mill's Rd. Cemetery

Bogtown Rd.

Cat Ridge Rd.

Turkey Hill Rd.

Hawley Mtn. Rd.

Route 121

Yerkes Rd.

NORTH

Todd Rd.

North Salem Rd. (Rte. 121/124)

Getting There

The ride's starting point is directly adjacent to exit 7 off I–684. Metro North provides railroad service from New York's Grand Central Station to Purdys, directly adjacent to the ride's starting point.

Route 35

Route 124

Ward Pound Ridge Reservation

DIREC-TIONS at a glance

0.0   Start at the intersection of Interstate 684, Route 22, and Route 116.

0.1   Right onto Route 116 east toward North Salem.

3.4   Left at triangle.

3.9   Left at stop sign onto Route 124.

4.3   Right onto Deveau Road.

4.9   At road's end, turn left to Hammond Museum. Afterward, head back down Deveau Road.

5.5   Left onto Route 124.

5.9   Right onto Route 116.

6.5   Left onto Routes 116/121.

7.0   Balanced Rock on right. Afterward, turn around.

7.5   Turn right onto Route 116 west (or continue on Route 121 south to Route 35 west and Route 124 south to Ward Pound Ridge Reservation).

8.6   Left onto Turkey Hill Road.

8.7   Right onto Mill's Road.

10.5 Right at stop sign to stay on Mill's Road.

11.0 Right onto Titicus River Road.

12.2 Left onto Route 22 to the beginning of the ride.

soon appear through the trees on the right. The reservoir supplies water to New York City, while its shoreline supplies cyclists with a wonderful natural setting.

At the reservoir's east end, continue on Route 116 as Turkey Hill Road intersects from the right. You will soon pass Salem Center, the site of the North Salem Town Hall in the town's **historic district**. Next door is the Delancy House (built in 1770) and a monument honoring the fallen soldiers of World War I.

Turn left at the four-way intersection with Route 124 (June Road). Just up the road on the left is the June Cemetery. Within its walls are headstones that date back to 1806.

After you pass the cemetery, get ready to turn right onto Deveau Road. Although it extends for only 0.6 mile, Deveau is the most challenging part of the ride, thanks to a steep profile and rugged surface. You might find it easier just to walk its length. Deveau, a dead-end street, stops at the entrance to the **Hammond Museum**. The museum, open Wednesday through Sunday afternoon, features beautifully landscaped gardens and elegantly furnished rooms. There is a small charge for admission.

Head back down Deveau (careful—remember the bumps) to Route 124. Turn left and backtrack to the intersection with Route 116; take another left. Just beyond the intersection is the Saint James Episcopal Church, in use since 1750.

Follow Route 116 left (east) as it joins Route 121 toward North Salem. In about 0.5 mile you will come to a most curious sight: **Balanced Rock**. According to a nearby sign, the rock—which is actually a ninety-ton boulder perched atop five smaller rocks—is a relic of the most recent ice age. Not everyone agrees with this theory, however. A different school of thought calls it a dolmen or stone table. In his book *America, B.C.* (Quadrangle Press, 1976), Barry Fell likens Balanced Rock to many similar rock formations found in New England, as well as northern Europe, that are thought to have been created by ancient civilizations such as the Celts or the Iberians, long before the birth of Christ. Balanced Rock is the largest example of a dolmen yet found in North America. While Fell's evidence is not totally compelling, it makes interesting food for thought.

Backtrack again to the intersection of Routes 116 and 121. If you wish to double the ride's length, continue straight on Route 121 south. In about 6 miles Route 121 will have wound its way toward the entrance of the **Ward Pound Ridge Reservation**. This 4,700-acre park boasts facilities for hiking, swimming, and picnicking. It is a wonderful place to spend the day or an entire weekend. Open-faced lean-tos are available for camping year-round (tents are not permitted). If you have always yearned to try bicycle camping but don't want to travel too far from home, Pound Ridge Reservation is the place to go. Afterward, return along Route 121 north to the intersection with Route 116.

To continue back toward Purdys, follow Route 116 to the west. After passing the North Salem Town Hall (this time on the right), turn left onto Turkey Hill Road and then right onto Mill's Road. Both begin with lovely open farmland. As Mill's Road continues to roll across hill and dale, the pastoral expanses give way to the wooded south shore of Titicus Reservoir.

About 0.3 mile after the right-hand turn at the Bogtown Road intersection, watch for the **Mill's Road Cemetery** on the left. Dating back to 1784, this small cemetery is immaculately maintained by the North Salem Historical Society.

Not far beyond the cemetery, turn right onto Titicus River Road. After a quick drop-off, the road takes you back to Routes 22 and 116.

For Further Information

Hammond Museum (914) 669–5135
Ward Pound Ridge Reservation (914) 763–3993

Putnam County, New York
The Putnam Panic!

Mileage:	35
Terrain:	Extremely hilly.
Traffic:	Light, except moderate near Lake Mahopac
Facilities:	Water, a concession stand, and rest rooms at Canopus Beach, near the beginning of the ride; food and drink available at the Adams Corner General Store at the corner of Church and Peekskill Hollow Roads.
Things to see:	Clarence Fahnestock Memorial State Park, Appalachian Trail, Lake Mahopac, West Branch Reservoir, Boyd Corners Reservoir

If you are looking for a real cycling challenge, you'll find it here in Putnam County. This is an extremely difficult ride, and should be attempted only by experienced riders; it is not for the casual weekend pedaler. Even riders in top condition will find these 35 miles to be the most demanding in this book. But what's life without a little challenge, right?

Begin the ride at the intersection of State Route 301 and the Taconic State Parkway, heading west on Route 301, in the midst of 6,800-acre **Clarence Fahnestock Memorial State Park**. Although there are no parking lots immediately adjacent to the departure point, there are plenty of spots available about 0.5 mile to the west on Route 301.

The ride starts out innocently enough with a pleasant down-hill coast toward Canopus Lake, one of the prime attractions within Fahnestock State Park. There, you'll find boat rentals, swimming, and camping, as well as hiking along the **Appalachian Trail**, which winds diagonally through much of the park. If you own a mountain bike, or just like hiking, you might even be tempted to try a little of the trail yourself. You'll cross paths with the trail again several miles ahead on Canopus Hollow Road.

Leaving Canopus Lake behind, the road starts up the ride's first major climb. Though not terribly steep, this hill lasts close to 2 miles before finally leveling off and starting to reverse its direction. As you begin to descend, turn left onto Canopus Hollow Road and get ready for a 5-mile plunge. By far the nicest part of the ride, hill-wise, Canopus Hollow passes through untouched woodlands sprinkled with an occasional house and side road.

At the end of Canopus Hollow Road, bear right onto Oscawana Lake Road (County Route 20), then left onto Church Road (County Route 22). Church climbs for about half of its 2-mile length, then descends into Adams Corners, where the Adams Corner General Store offers welcome relief to wearied cyclists.

Turn left onto Peekskill Hollow Road for the 3-mile, flat-to-rolling ride to Bryant Pond Road, where a red barn and horse farm mark the corner. Turn right and get ready to charge up the ride's toughest climb. Though it lasts only 1 mile, Bryant Pond Road is a murderous ascent, steep and curvy—a truly challenging combination. Bryant Pond itself greets you through the trees on the left as you approach the top. Then, take a look over your shoulder at the warning sign facing the opposite direction: HILL. You'll think, "No kidding!"

Follow the route to the left, circling Bryant Pond, as it continues onto Barger Road. Ride over the Taconic State, then cross Wood Street (County Route 24) to end up on Secor Road (County Route 30). Fortunately, Secor Road goes more or less downhill—a most welcome relief from the hills just left behind. At its end, turn left onto State Route 6N and continue downhill for a ways. But remember: Whatever goes down, must go up, and Route 6N is no

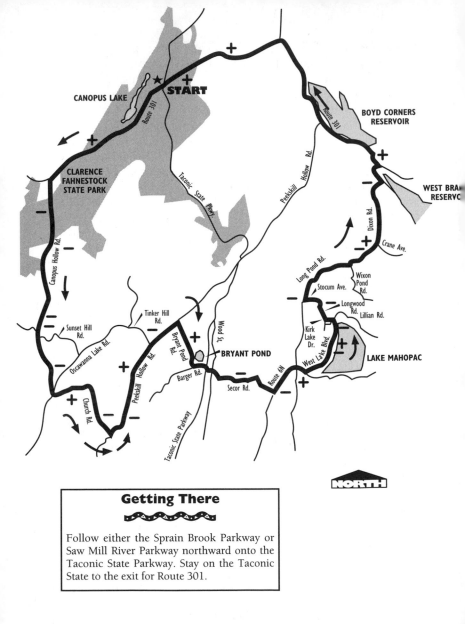

CANOPUS LAKE

★ START

BOYD CORNERS RESERVOIR

Route 301

Route 301

CLARENCE FAHNESTOCK STATE PARK

WEST BRA RESERVO

Peekskill Hollow Rd.

Taconic State Pkwy.

Canopus Hollow Rd.

Dixon Rd.

Crane Ave.

Long Pond Rd.

Wixon Pond Rd.

Stocum Ave.

Longwood Rd.

Lillian Rd.

Tinker Hill Rd.

Sunset Hill Rd.

Oscawanna Lake Rd.

Peekskill Hollow Rd.

Bryant Pond Rd.

Wood St.

BRYANT POND

Kirk Lake Dr.

West Lake Blvd.

LAKE MAHOPAC

Barger Rd.

Secor Rd.

Route 6N

Church Rd.

Taconic State Parkway

NORTH

Getting There

Follow either the Sprain Brook Parkway or Saw Mill River Parkway northward onto the Taconic State Parkway. Stay on the Taconic State to the exit for Route 301.

DIREC-TIONS
at a glance

0.0   Start at the intersection of Route 301 (Cold Spring Turnpike) and the Taconic State Parkway. Head west on Route 301.

3.6   Turn left onto Canopus Hollow Road.

9.0   Turn right onto Oscawana Lake Road (County Route 20).

9.1   Turn left onto Church Road (County Route 22).

11.3   Turn left onto Peekskill Hollow Road (County Route 21).

14.3   Turn right onto Bryant Pond Road.

15.2   Veer left onto Barger Road.

15.8   Continue straight across Wood Street onto Secor Road (County Route 30).

17.4   Turn left onto State Route 6N.

18.6   Turn left onto West Lake Boulevard

20.2   Turn left onto Lillian Road.

20.3   Veer left to stay on Lillian Road

20.4   Turn right onto Kirk Lake Drive.

21.0   Turn left onto Stocum Avenue.

21.4   Turn right onto Long Pond Road.

23.8   Turn left onto Dixon Pond Road.

25.8   Turn left onto State Route 301.

34.5   Back at starting point.

exception as it climbs toward the intersection with West Lake Boulevard, where the ride takes a left.

Though narrow and somewhat overcrowded with cars, West Lake offers a spectacular view of **Lake Mahopac**. In the summer, you are likely to see anything from swimming, boating, and fishing to parasailing but take care not to get so distracted that you ignore the road!

Just around a sharp turn to the right, take a left onto Lillian Road. This is followed by a right onto Kirk Lake Drive, as you wind your way along the shore of Kirk Lake. Turn left onto Stocum Avenue, crossing a small bridge over the lake's northern tip, then bear right onto Long Pond Road (County Route 32).

Happily, though it has its ups and downs, Long Pond Road features an overall downhill slope.

Not long after passing Long Pond on the right, turn left at the Mahopac Volunteer Fire Department onto Dixon Road. Dixon is characterized by lots of short-but-steep ups and downs (mostly downs), resulting in a roller-coaster–like ride and ending at the northern tip of the **West Branch Reservoir.**

With all these downhills, you must be rested up from the earlier climbs, right? Hope so, because with the left turn onto Route 301, it's time to head back up to Fahnestock State Park. And we do mean up! Though there are some dips along the way, Route 301 maintains its upward profile over the entire 9 miles back to the ride's starting point. Having said that, we advise that you set a slow pace and enjoy the view of **Boyd Corners Reservoir** through the trees on the right. This is one of several reservoirs in the county that help supply New York City with its drinking water.

Follow Route 301 around a sharp turn to the left for the final sprint back to the starting point. As you cross the bridge over the Taconic State Parkway, you should feel satisfied knowing that you have conquered a truly difficult course. But satisfaction can wait; right now find someplace soft to sit down and collapse! WHEW!

For Further Information

Clarence Fahnestock Memorial State Park (914) 225–7207

Rockland County, New York

Hudson River Loop

Mileage:	26
Terrain:	Rolling to extremely hilly
Traffic:	Light to moderate
Facilities:	Water and rest rooms in the nature center adjacent to field #1 in Rockland Lake State Park as well as in the West Nyack Public Library on Strawtown Road; delis at the corner of Cristian Herald and Rockland Lake Roads, and on Broadway near Highmount Road in Nyack; a bakery on the corner of Broadway and High Avenue in Nyack must be very popular with cyclists, judging by the number of bike racks nearby
Things to see:	Hudson River, Rockland Lake State Park, Tappan Zee Bridge, Onderdonk House, Blauvelt Interstate Park, Johannes Blauvelt Homestead, Clarksville Inn, Lake De Forest

The **Hudson River** is considered one of the most beautiful rivers in the country, if not the world. Touring its banks by bicycle offers some outstanding scenery and some spectacular challenges.

Begin from parking field #1 at **Rockland Lake State Park,** one of a chain of parks that make up the Palisades Interstate Park System. Exiting through the park's south exit, continue straight across Route 9

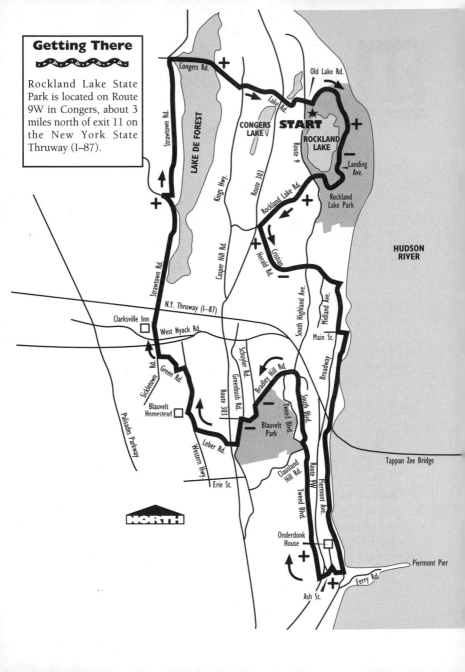

Getting There

Rockland Lake State Park is located on Route 9W in Congers, about 3 miles north of exit 11 on the New York State Thruway (I–87).

Congers Rd.

Old Lake Rd.

Lake Rd.

Strawtown Rd.

LAKE DE FOREST

CONGERS LAKE

START

Route 9

ROCKLAND LAKE

Landing Ave.

Rockland Lake Park

Kings Hwy.

Route 303

Rockland Lake Rd.

Casper Hill Rd.

Cristian

Herald Rd.

HUDSON RIVER

N.Y. Thruway (I–87)

Strawtown Rd.

Clarksville Inn

West Nyack Rd.

Sickletown Rd.

Green Rd.

Schuyler Rd.

Greenbush Rd.

Route 303

Bradley Hill Rd.

South Highland Ave.

Midland Ave.

Main St.

Broadway

Blauvelt Homestead

Tweed Blvd.

South Blvd.

Blauvelt Park

Leber Rd.

Western Hwy.

Palisades Parkway

Erie St.

Clausland Hill Rd.

Route 9W

Tweed Blvd.

Piermont Ave.

Tappan Zee Bridge

NORTH

Onderdonk House

Piermont Pier

Ash St.

Ferry Rd.

DIREC- TIONS at a glance

0.0	Right out of parking field #1 in Rockland Lake State Park.
1.0	Right at T onto Landing Avenue.
2.5	Leave park at south exit and cross Route 9W onto Rockland Lake Road.
3.7	Left onto Cristian Herald Road.
4.8	Cross Route 9W onto Old Mountain Road.
5.6	Right onto Broadway.
6.4	Left onto Ackerman Place.
6.5	Right onto Gedney Street.
6.7	Right onto Main Street.
6.8	Left onto Piermont Avenue.
10.2	Right onto Ash Street.
10.7	Left onto Route 9.
10.8	Right onto Tweed Boulevard.
13.1	Right onto South Boulevard. Go straight for gravelly shortcut through Blauvelt Park.
14.0	Left onto South Highland Avenue.
14.2	Right onto Bradley Hill Road (unmarked).
15.6	Left onto Greenbush Road.
15.9	Cross Route 303 onto Leber Road. (See note in text.)
16.0	At T continue to the right on Leber.
16.7	Right onto Western Highway.
17.7	Left onto Green Road.
18.4	Right onto County Route 23 (Sickletown Road/ Strawtown Road).
23.2	Right onto Congers Road (County Route 80).
24.5	Follow County Route 80 (now called Lake Road) through Congers.
25.5	Follow County Route 80 to the left onto Old Lake Road.
25.6	Cross Route 9W to Rockland Lake State Park.

onto Rockland Lake Road. Though it climbs at first, Rockland Lake Road is mostly flat. At its end turn sharply to the left onto Cristian Herald Road. Cristian Herald presents the first real challenge of the ride as it is up, up, and away for nearly 0.75 mile.

At the end of Cristian Herald Road, continue straight across Route 9W onto Old Mountain Road. Try not to build up too much speed going down the old mountain, because at its bottom, around a sharp right turn, Old Mountain Road shoots off to the left. If you are going too fast, you will miss the intersection (we have!) and end up on Midland Avenue.

Old Mountain Road ends at a T intersection with Broadway. Turning right, our route now travels southward along the Hudson's west bank. In between the road and the river are many stately homes. There is also a nice deli down the road on the right if you want to stop for a quick refueling or to pick up lunch. Broadway is marked with many green-and-white BIKE ROUTE signs, which will help you navigate through the center of Nyack in the miles to come.

Following the posted bike route, turn left onto Ackerman Place and take a fast plunge down toward the river. Then take two quick rights and a left to wind up on Piermont Avenue. Piermont is a long, flat stretch that runs right along the Hudson.

About a mile later, pass under the **Tappan Zee Bridge** and enter the village of Grand-View-On-Hudson. Many Victorian homes line the street, reflecting the glory of a bygone era.

As you approach the center of Piermont, keep an eye out for Ritie Street. On the corner is a bronze plaque marking the **Onderdonk House.** This was the 1783 site where George Washington met with leaders of the British army and where Britain first officially recognized the United States as an independent nation.

As you enter Piermont you have the option of continuing straight to Tallman Mountain State Park or turning left to the Piermont Pier. Our route, however, bears right and heads up Ash Street. And we do mean up! Ash is an incredible climb that is best walked.

At the fork up ahead, follow Ash to the left onto Route 9W, followed by a quick right onto Tweed Boulevard—drat, uphill again!

Happily, you can put away the mountain-climbing gear as the hill crests; Tweed is mostly flat from here on. Take our word for it, the views of the Hudson will have made the climb worth it.

Tweed Boulevard ends at a four-way intersection with Clausland Hill Road. It is now decision time. Straight ahead is the road into **Blauvelt Interstate Park**. Unfortunately, the park road shortly changes to gravel. If you have a mountain bike, it might be an exciting diversion; proceed all the way through to Bradley Hill Road.

If you choose the smoother route, take a right onto Clausland, which later changes to South Boulevard. Turn left onto South Highland Avenue and then right onto unmarked Bradley Hill Road. Bradley Hill offers abundant shade, and for once the road is going in the right direction—downhill.

Continue until you reach a four-way intersection with Greenbush Road; turn left. Cross Route 303 onto Leber Road. Follow Leber to the right after crossing a railroad bridge and continue all the way to the road's end at Western Highway, where you will turn right. (*Note:* As of mid-1998, the railroad bridge was closed for repairs. Until it is reopened, turn left onto Route 303 to Erie Street. Turn right onto Erie, travel up a hill, then turn right to join Western Highway. This detour adds about 1 mile to the ride.) About 0.5 mile after joining Western Highway, watch for a historical marker in front of a Dutch farmhouse on the left. This is the **Johannes Blauvelt Homestead**, site of the first U.S. tobacco company.

The route next turns left onto Green Road and then right onto Sickletown Road (County Route 23). Just ahead on the left is a marker pointing to **Clarksville Inn**, an early stagecoach stop. Continuing north on County Route 23 (now called Strawtown Road), watch for the first signs of **Lake De Forest** to the east, just before the road makes a sharp right-hand turn. You will get a much better view of this beautiful body of water as you approach the intersection with Congers Road (County Route 80).

Follow County Route 80 east all the way into Congers. Although the road changes names to Lake Road and later Old Lake Road, stay on it through town. Popping out the other side of the town, you will come to Route 9W and the north entrance of Rockland Lake State Park. Welcome back.

For Further Information

Rockland Lake State Park (914) 268–3020 or (914) 268–7598
Clarksville Inn (914) 358–8899

Rockland County, New York

Stony Point

Mileage:	9 (23, with optional side trip to Bear Mountain State Park)
Terrain:	Hilly
Traffic:	Moderate
Facilities:	Food store at Stony Ridge Plaza, the ride's starting point; water and rest room facilities in the Tomkins Cover Library on Route 9W, just before Mott Farm Road, as well as in Stony Point State Park
Things to see:	Buckberg Mountain, Springsteel Farm marker, Bear Mountain State Park (optional), Stony Point State Park

Lying south of Bear Mountain State Park, the village of Stony Point is a serene hamlet blessed with a commanding view of the Hudson River. In colonial days Stony Point served as the western landing for a cross-river ferry that shuttled traffic over to Verplanck's Point on the eastern shore. The ferry was a vital link connecting New England with New Jersey, Pennsylvania, and the southern colonies.

In an effort to sever this all-important trade route during the Revolutionary War, British troops seized Stony Point on May 30, 1779. By this capture, Sir Henry Clinton, commander of the British force, also successfully cut off General George Washington and the Continental Army from New York City.

Washington, realizing the importance of Stony Point, called in General Anthony Wayne to mastermind a plan to rid the town of the

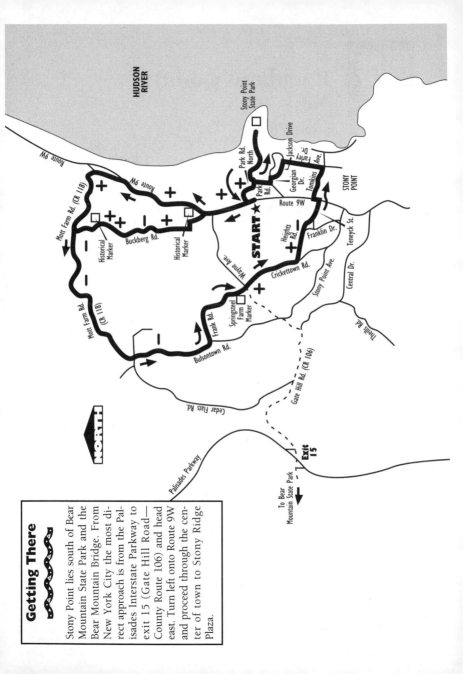

Getting There

Stony Point lies south of Bear Mountain State Park and the Bear Mountain Bridge. From New York City the most direct approach is from the Palisades Interstate Parkway to exit 15 (Gate Hill Road—County Route 106) and head east. Turn left onto Route 9W and proceed through the center of town to Stony Ridge Plaza.

NORTH

HUDSON RIVER

Route 9W

Mott Farm Rd. (CR 118)

Route 9W

Buckberg Rd.

Historical Marker

Historical Marker

Mott Farm Rd. (CR 118)

Frank Rd.

Springsteel Farm Marker

Bulsontown Rd.

Cedar Flats Rd.

Palisades Parkway

Gate Hill Rd. (CR 106)

Exit 15

To Bear Mountain State Park

Wayne Ave.

Crickettown Rd.

START

Route 9W

Heights Rd.

Franklin Dr.

Stony Point Ave.

Central Dr.

Thiells Rd.

Teneyck St.

STONY POINT

Georgian Dr.

Tomkins

Farley Dr.

Jackson Drive

Park Rd.

Park Rd. North

Stony Point State Park

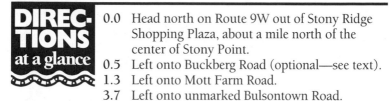

DIREC-TIONS at a glance

0.0	Head north on Route 9W out of Stony Ridge Shopping Plaza, about a mile north of the center of Stony Point.
0.5	Left onto Buckberg Road (optional—see text).
1.3	Left onto Mott Farm Road.
3.7	Left onto unmarked Bulsontown Road.

4.5 Left onto Frank Road.

5.4 Straight onto Crickettown Road.

5.9 Left onto Heights Road.

6.4 Left onto Teneyck Street.

6.6 Left onto Route 9W; then right onto Tomkins Avenue.

6.9 Left onto Farley Drive.

7.2 Left onto Jackson Drive.

7.5 Left onto Georgian Drive.

7.6 Right onto Park Road. Continue into state park.

8.8 Exit park on Park Road North. Continue to end at Route 9W, then turn left.

9.1 Back at Stony Ridge Plaza.

British Army. "Mad Anthony," so nicknamed for the apparent reck-lessness of the Stony Point campaign, was given full charge of more than 1,500 light infantrymen for the battle. You are about to trace much of the route used by Wayne and his troops as they fought to re-capture Stony Point.

Depart from the Stony Ridge Plaza, located on Route 9W about a mile north of town. Head north on Route 9W. In 0.5 mile you will pass Buckberg Road on the left. A small marker on the corner in-forms passersby that this was once an important military route that ran all the way to West Point. If you like mountain climbing, you can continue on this road as it heads up and over **Buckberg Mountain.**

A second historical marker, farther up Buckberg Road on the right, indicates the site where Washington and Wayne surveyed the British encampment at Stony Point while plotting a strategy for the

attack. None of the trees and brush that block the river view today existed two centuries ago (they were all brought in earlier this century by homeowners and developers). From atop this rocky knoll, the generals had a clear view of the enemy's actions.

If you want to avoid the climb over Buckberg Mountain, stay on northbound Route 9W into Tomkins Cove and turn left onto Mott Farm Road (County Route 118). Although Mott Farm begins with an uphill climb, it is still the lesser of two evils. Besides, in only a mile or so it begins a long, pleasant downhill run. Up ahead, at a T intersection, turn left onto unmarked Bulsontown Road and continue downhill.

The hill continues beyond the left turn you must take onto Frank Road, so be sure not to zip right by. Be on the lookout for overhead high-voltage wires; you pass under them just before the turn. Frank Road (sometimes spelled *Franck*) dates to pre-Revolutionary times, when it extended over the Ramapo Mountains. It was along Frank Road, at the **Springsteel Farm**, that Wayne and his squad assembled before they broke for the attack on Stony Point. Though the farm is long gone, a handmade **marker** hidden in the woods on the right across from Boy Scout Camp Bulowa marks the site of the farmhouse.

Wayne split his troops into three large divisions. One was to attack from the north, one from the south, and the third directly from the west. The troops left the farm just before midnight, traveling southward on Frank Road. At the next intersection (now known as Wayne Avenue), the northern division split off to the left, while the others continued on Crickettown Road, just as you will.

Before proceeding down Crickettown, you may wish to extend the ride into nearby **Bear Mountain State Park.** (This sidetrip will add 14 miles to your route.) If so, follow Wayne Avenue to the right all the way to its end at Gate Hill Road (County Route 106). Turn right onto Gate Hill and continue into the park. Mile after mile of pleasant (albeit hilly) cycling await anyone who roams into the park. For more information on the park's roads, trails, and other features, call the park information office at the telephone number listed at the end of this ride.

Back on track with General Wayne, continue on Crickettown Road to Heights Road, where the route bears left just before a steep downgrade. Follow a zigzag path through town on Teneyck Street to Route 9W and finally onto Tomkins Avenue. Though Wayne's men assaulted the point by moving right along the river's edge, the bike route follows a somewhat drier approach. Bear left onto Farley Drive and weave your way onto Jackson, then Georgian, followed by a right onto Park Road. Take this all the way to **Stony Point State Park.**

Upon entering the park, dismount your bike next to the museum entrance and step inside to finish the story of the battle. As the exhibits explain, Wayne and his troops successfully recaptured Stony Point from the British in less than an hour, though not without cost. Fifteen Americans were killed and eighty-three wounded, while the British suffered twenty casualties and seventy-four wounded. Many mementos on display in the museum remain as a testimony to the bravery of the soldiers who fought to secure our young country's freedom. Maps are available that guide visitors along the park's footpaths past many of the battle's key sites. Of special interest is the location of the Britishers' main redoubt perched atop a rock outcropping at the highest tip of the point. The park is open Wednesday through Sunday from 8:30 A.M. to 5:00 P.M.

Return from the park as you entered, along Park Road. Turn right onto Park Road North and continue to its end at Route 9W. Bear left and return to the shopping center from which you began. Congratulations—you, too, have conquered Stony Point.

For Further Information

Bear Mountain State Park (914) 786–2701
Stony Point State Park (914) 786–2521

Orange County, New York

Monroe to Chester

Mileage:	16
Terrain:	Moderately hilly
Traffic:	Light
Facilities:	Several food stores along Route 17M, adjacent to the starting point; restaurants and a deli in Sugar Loaf Village; water and rest rooms available at the Chester Public Library and Museum Village
Things to see:	Round Lake, Walton Lake, Sugar Loaf Village, Museum Village

In many ways, residents of Orange County have the best of both worlds. On one hand, they bask in beautiful rural surroundings of farms, pastures, and small towns. On the other, they enjoy easy access to New York City, which lies a scant 40 miles down the Hudson River. You are about to tour some of the county's loveliest lakes, farms, and meadows. Along the way you can choose to visit two villages that are unlike any others in the tristate region.

From the center of Monroe, pedal south on Lake Road (County Route 5). About 0.25 mile along on the left, watch for a small pond fed by a charming little waterfall. A waterwheel stands ready for action, but its weathered face seems to say that it has lain dormant for years.

Even though its shoulders are narrow, Lake Road is great for bicycling. And it certainly is appropriately named, as you are about to discover. Just over the next hill, **Round Lake**, one of two large bodies of

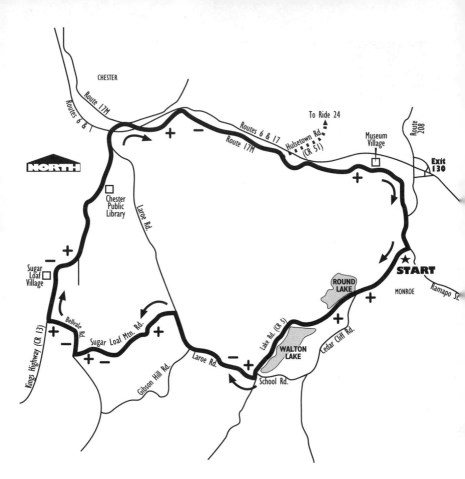

CHESTER

Route 17M

Routes 6 & 1

Routes 6 & 17

Route 17M

To Ride 24

Hulsetown Rd.
(CR 51)

Museum
Village

Route 208

Exit
130

NORTH

Chester Public
Library

Laroe Rd.

★ START

Sugar
Loaf
Village

ROUND
LAKE

MONROE

Ramapo St.

Bellvale Rd.

Sugar Loaf Mtn. Rd.

Lake Rd. (CR 5)

Kings Highway (CR 13)

Gibson Hill Rd.

Laroe Rd.

WALTON
LAKE

Cedar Cliff Rd.

School Rd.

Getting There

Take the New York Thruway (Interstate 87) to
Routes 6 and 17 (exit 16). Proceed west to exit
130, then south on Route 208 to Route 17M.
Follow 17M into the center of Monroe.

DIREC-TIONS at a glance

0.0 Head south on Lake Road (County Route 5) from Route 17M away from the center of Monroe.

3.1 Right onto Laroe Road.

4.6 Left onto Sugar Loaf Mountain Road.

6.3 Right onto Bellvale Road.

7.0 Right onto Kings Highway (County Route 13).

8.0 Left to stay on Kings Highway.

10.3 Right onto Route 17M heading east.

15.7 Back at the corner of Lake Road and Route 17M.

water along this road, greets you on the right. The small park along the shore of Round Lake is a perfect place to pull over for a roadside picnic.

Continue down Lake Road along the water's edge; be careful, as the road is narrow in spots. A second hill lies between Round Lake and **Walton Lake**. Once ascended, however, the peak provides a nice view of the lake and its beautiful environment.

Just past the southern tip of Walton Lake, turn right onto Laroe Road. Though it begins with a mild uphill notch, Laroe quickly changes profile to a long, downhill run that lasts for nearly 1.5 miles. Close to the bottom, turn left onto Sugar Loaf Mountain Road. While it is less than 2 miles long, this is the toughest stretch of road on the entire ride. The first half is especially challenging. If you are like us, though, the pain in your legs will be tempered by the scenic beauty of the area.

Sugar Loaf Mountain Road ends at unmarked Bellvale Road, where the ride turns right. The barns and silos seen in the distance clearly show that much of Orange County is still agricultural.

A right turn onto Kings Highway (County Route 13) takes you into the magical village of **Sugar Loaf**. This wonderful town has more than fifty small shops where talented artisans display and sell their handmade crafts. Stores of all sorts line Kings Highway, with many

dating back to the town's origin in 1749. Among our favorites is Grandma Pat's Doll Museum. Three thousand dolls from around the world and across various time periods line Grandma's walls. Nearby, the Exposures Gallery features original photographic art that is truly one of a kind. Another unique shop is Basic Blue, with a marvelous collection of kaleidoscopes, chess sets, and cards. If all this has made you hungry, stop by one of the many food emporiums in town. They range from formal restaurants to a pizzeria, a deli, and Joan's Cones (an ice cream parlor). Need we say more?

Several special events are held at Sugar Loaf annually. Among these are the Spring Festival on Memorial Day weekend, an antique car show in August, and the Fall Festival in October. Concerts are held during the warmer months; call ahead for the schedule.

Beyond Sugar Loaf the road slides down a small hill, crosses the railroad tracks, then turns left at a T intersection to ascend past many acres of open farmland. Kings Highway soon flattens out for the 2-mile trek toward Chester. At Route 17M the ride continues to the right, but if you need to touch civilization (for food, rest rooms, etc.), turn left to enter the town itself.

As you head east on Route 17M, the pastoral surroundings continue on the right side of the road; on your left are heavily traveled Routes 6 and 17. The contrast is striking! After climbing a rather long hill, prepare yourself for the longest downhill run of the ride. This is just what the doctor ordered for a hot summer's day! (If it's a nice day, why not extend the ride into nearby Goshen and Washingtonville? Turn left near the bottom of the hill onto Hulsetown Road—County Route 51—for the 5-mile trip to pick up Ride #24.)

The slope of the road reverses itself as you approach **Museum Village** on the left. The village is an authentic re-creation of a colonial town dating to about 1800. Within, you can visit a blacksmith's shop, schoolhouse, general store, and more than twenty other exhibition buildings. Many feature live demonstrations by villagers dressed in authentic period garb. Museum Village is open Wednesdays through Sundays from May to December. There is a charge for admission.

From here it's just a short trip back into Monroe. If you wish, follow the green-and-white BIKE ROUTE sign across the road at the intersection with Route 208. It leads to a paved bike lane that is completely separated from the busy street. Farther along, the path winds through a lovely town park encircling Mill Pond. Be watchful of the many pedestrians that also use the path. In just 0.5 mile you will be back at Lake Road but you may prefer to continue touring the park on your own.

For Further Information

Village of Sugar Loaf (914) 469–4963
Museum Village (914) 782–8247

Orange County, New York

Goshen to Washingtonville

Mileage:	22
Terrain:	Rolling to hilly
Traffic:	Light
Facilities:	Food available from a deli at the corner of Sarah Wells Trail and Route 208, as well as in the center of Washingtonville; fast food in Washingtonville, to the right on Route 94 (about 0.1 mile off the bike route), rest rooms and water (and wine!) at the Brotherhood Winery, as well as at a town park on Craigville Road (about halfway between Hasbrouck Road and Main Street) and at the Goshen Public Library in the middle of town
Things to see:	Historic Track, Trotting Horse Museum, Brotherhood Winery

Like the previous route, this ride takes cyclists through pastureland and woodland, touching a bit of American history along the way. We begin at the intersection of Church Street and Main Street (Route 207) in Goshen. Founded in 1714, the town has been the county seat since 1727. The pride that Goshen takes in its rich heritage is immediately apparent as you look around its central green. West of the green is the imposing façade of the Goshen United Methodist Church, while to its south is the majestic First Presbyterian Church of Goshen.

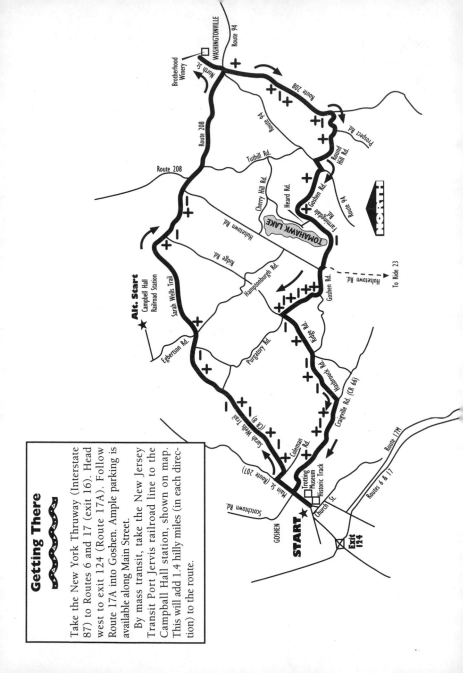

Getting There

Take the New York Thruway (Interstate 87) to Routes 6 and 17 (exit 16). Head west to exit 124 (Route 17A). Follow Route 17A into Goshen. Ample parking is available along Main Street.

By mass transit, take the New Jersey Transit Port Jervis railroad line to the Campball Hall station, shown on map. This will add 1.4 hilly miles (in each direction) to the route.

NORTH

WASHINGTONVILLE

Route 94

Brotherhood Winery

North St.

Route 208

Route 208

Route 94

Route 208

Tuthill Rd.

Cherry Hill Rd.

Heard Rd.

Hulsetown Rd.

Ridge Rd.

Sarah Wells Trail

Egbertson Rd.

Campbell Hall Railroad Station

Alt. Start

Hamptonburgh Rd.

Purgatory Rd.

Sarah Wells Trail (CR 8)

Coleman Rd.

Main St. (Route 207)

Scotchtown Rd.

GOSHEN

START

Trotting Museum

Historic Track

Church St.

Exit 124

Route 6 & 17

Route 17M

Craigville Rd. (CR 66)

Hatbrouck Rd.

Ridge Rd.

Goshen Rd.

Goshen Rd.

Fanningdale Rd.

Round Hill Rd.

Prospect Rd.

Route 208

Route 94

TOMAHAWK LAKE

Hulsetown Rd.

To Ride 23

0.0	Begin at Goshen green at intersection with Main Street (Route 207) and Church Street.
1.0	Right onto Sarah Wells Trail (County Route 8).
1.1	Bear left to stay on Sarah Wells Trail.
7.6	Right onto Route 208.
9.7	Left onto Route 94 in center of Washingtonville.
9.8	Left onto North Street.
10.0	Right into Brotherhood Winery; turn around and return on North Street.
10.3	Right onto East Main Street (Route 94).
10.4	Left onto Route 208 (south).
12.7	Right onto Round Hill Road.
13.0	Right to stay on Round Hill Road.
13.8	Left onto Route 94.
13.9	Right onto Goshen Road, later changes to Farmingdale Road.
16.1	Cross Hulsetown Road and continue on Goshen Road (name change again!).
16.7	Right at stop sign onto Purgatory Road.
17.5	Left at stop sign to stay on Ridge Road.
18.4	Right at stop sign onto Hasbrouck Road.
19.4	Right onto Craigville Road (County Route 66).
21.3	Left at stop sign onto Main Street (Route 207).
21.8	Back at green.

Several monuments around the green commemorate events and citizens important to local history. One of the more unusual is a special streetlight found at the corner of Church and Main. At the base of the lamp, four sculpted black horses' heads commemorate the town's involvement with horse breeding and racing. Indeed, Goshen has been nicknamed the "cradle of the trotter."

North of the green, past the intersection with Park Place (on the right), stands one of the world's oldest harness-racing tracks. **Historic Track** has seen many racing firsts since it opened in the 1840s, including the first sub-two-minute mile by a trotter and the first half-mile track to join the Grand Circuit. More recently, the track became the sporting world's first national historic site.

Historic Track's rich past is well documented in the **Trotting Horse Museum** at 240 Main Street. Racing memorabilia, Currier and Ives prints, and more than 100 displays await visitors. The museum is open daily from 10:00 A.M. (noon on Sunday and holidays) until 5:00 P.M., and there is a small admission charge.

On the track side of Main Street, known as "Lawyers Row," are several beautifully maintained vintage homes. One of the more noteworthy is #210, a red-brick dwelling. There, in 1873, President Ulysses S. Grant stayed overnight to watch the races.

Leave Goshen on northbound Main Street and turn right onto Sarah Wells Trail (County Route 8) in about a mile. Miss Wells was the first European woman to settle in Goshen township in 1714. Her home was situated about 3 miles ahead on the right, though no trace of it exists nowadays.

While the trail begins in a typical suburban neighborhood, the homes are quickly replaced by cows and rolling pastures as you leave the town behind. There is one home, however, that is bound to attract your attention. To us it looks just like the South Fork ranch from the television series *Dallas*! You'll find it on the right at the top of a hill, about 3 miles after you turn onto the road (ironically, not far from where the humble Wells homestead once stood).

About a mile after you cross some railroad tracks, turn right onto Route 208. Follow this into Washingtonville, being especially careful of the bumps in the road as you approach the town's center. Take a left onto Route 94, followed almost immediately by another left onto North Street. **The Brotherhood Winery** awaits about 0.25 mile ahead on the right.

Brotherhood, which was founded in 1839, is America's oldest winery. If you have the time, why not join one of the guided tours available daily? They take just over an hour to complete. Special events are scheduled throughout the year, including harvest and grape-stomping festivals. Wine sampling is also available to tour groups, but remember, you're riding!

Return to southbound Route 208 (now called South Street) and head out of Washingtonville. Though the road begins on the bumpy side, it becomes smoother when it enters more rural environs, just over a small rise.

In a little more than 2 miles, make a right onto Round Hill Road. Round Hill is characterized by rolling meadows peppered by a couple of short but steep climbs. At its end, turn left onto Route 94, then right (just beyond an antiques shop) onto Goshen Road. Goshen, which changes names to Farmingdale Road, then back again, is thickly wooded, with few homes. Though the road is a bit secluded, the shade is welcome, especially on hot summer afternoons.

Not long after passing Heard Road on the right, keep an eye out on the same side for the southern tip of Tomahawk Lake. Tomahawk is a lovely body of water set in a beautiful valley. If you want an even better view of the lake, turn right onto Heard Road and continue to its end; then backtrack to Farmingdale.

Cross Hulsetown Road (County Route 51) and continue straight on Goshen Road. (To extend the ride into nearby Chester and Monroe, follow Hulsetown to the left for 5 miles until it ends at Route 17M. There, pick up Ride #23.) Cross over the railroad tracks (careful, they are bumpy!) and begin a steep 0.5-mile climb. Turn right at the next stop sign onto Purgatory Road and begin a roller-coaster trek over hill and dale.

Take a left at the stop sign onto Ridge Road, passing more open meadow along the way. Shortly, at a four-way intersection, turn right onto unmarked Hasbrouck Road (Farmingdale Road intersects on the left). Hasbrouck begins with an uphill sprint but finishes with a long descent.

For the ride's final leg, turn right onto Craigville Road (County Route 66), followed by a left in 2 miles back onto Main Street (Route 207). From here it's only 0.5 mile to the center of Goshen.

For Further Information

Historic Track (914) 294–5333
Trotting Horse Museum (914) 294–6330
Brotherhood Winery (914) 496–9101

Fairfield County, Connecticut

Greenwich

Mileage:	21
Terrain:	Hilly
Traffic:	Mostly light
Facilities:	Rest rooms and water at the ride's beginning at the Bruce Museum and in Bruce Park (near playground); food supplies available from a convenience store at the corner of Indian Field Road and East Putnam Avenue (Route 1); food in Banksville, New York, located about 2 up-and-down miles north on North Avenue.
Things to see:	Bruce Museum, Bruce Park, River-bridge Park, Rockwood Lake, Putnam Reservoir, Radio marker, Civil War monument

For many New Yorkers Greenwich, Connecticut acts as the gateway to New England. But given that they live less than 40 miles from Times Square, most Greenwich residents probably align themselves more with the Big Apple than with, say, Boston. Greenwich offers an exquisite backdrop for many cycling adventures through the countryside. Here we offer just one possibility.

Depart from the intersection of Arch Street, Steamboat Road, Greenwich Avenue, and Museum Drive, proceeding eastward on the latter. Just up the hill on the left is a large mansion. The sign at its entrance tells you that this is the **Bruce Museum**. The museum features exhibits highlighting the arts and sciences. Inside, displays of paint-

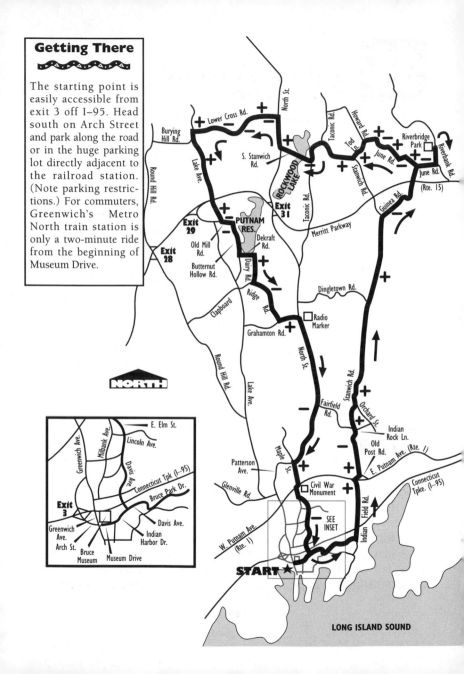

Getting There

The starting point is easily accessible from exit 3 off I–95. Head south on Arch Street and park along the road or in the huge parking lot directly adjacent to the railroad station. (Note parking restrictions.) For commuters, Greenwich's Metro North train station is only a two-minute ride from the beginning of Museum Drive.

NORTH

LONG ISLAND SOUND

Lower Cross Rd.
North St.
Burying Hill Rd.
S. Stanwich Rd.
Taconic Rd.
Howard Rd.
Tod Ln.
June Rd.
Riverbridge Park
Riverbank Rd.
June Rd. (Rte. 15)
ROCKWOOD LAKE
Stanwich Rd.
Exit 31
Taconic Rd.
Guinea Rd.
Merritt Parkway
Round Hill Rd.
Lake Ave.
Exit 29
PUTNAM RES.
Old Mill Rd.
Dekraft Rd.
Dairy Rd.
Exit 28
Butternut Hollow Rd.
Ridge Rd.
Dingletown Rd.
Clapboard
Grahamton Rd.
Radio Marker
North St.
Round Hill Rd.
Lake Ave.
Fairfield Rd.
Stanwich Rd.
Orchard St.
Indian Rock Ln.
Old Post Rd.
E. Putnam Ave. (Rte. 1)
Patterson Ave.
Maple St.
Civil War Monument
Glenville Rd.
Indian Field Rd.
Connecticut Tpke. (I-95)
W. Putnam Ave. (Rte. 1)
SEE INSET
START ★

E. Elm St.
Greenwich Ave.
Milbank Ave.
Lincoln Ave.
Davis Ave.
Connecticut Tpke. (I–95)
Bruce Park Dr.
Exit 3
Davis Ave.
Greenwich Ave.
Arch St.
Indian Harbor Dr.
Bruce Museum
Museum Drive

DIREC-TIONS at a glance

0.0	Begin at the corner of Museum Drive and Greenwich Avenue.
0.2	Left onto Indian Harbor Drive.
0.3	Straight onto Davis Avenue.
0.6	Left onto Bruce Park Drive.
1.1	Left onto Indian Field Drive.
2.0	Cross East Putnam Avenue (Route 1); follow Old Post Road to right.
2.1	Left onto Stanwich Road.
3.2	Left to stay on Stanwich Road.
6.2	Right onto Guinea Road.
7.3	Right onto June Road.
7.5	Left onto Riverbank Road.
7.6	Left into Riverbridge Park.
7.7	Right onto June Road.
7.9	Right to stay on June Road.
9.0	Left onto Tod Lane.
9.3	Right onto Stanwich Road.
9.9	Straight onto Taconic Road.
10.3	Right onto South Stanwich Road.
10.8	Right onto North Street.
11.3	Left onto Lower Cross Road.
12.7	Left onto Lake Avenue.
14.1	Left onto Old Mill Road.
14.3	Right onto Butternut Hollow Road.
14.9	Left onto Dekraft Road.
15.2	Right onto Dairy Road.
15.5	Left onto Clapboard Ridge Road.
16.3	Left to stay on Clapboard Ridge Road.
16.6	Right onto North Street.
19.0	Left onto Maple Street.
19.3	Right onto East Putnam Avenue; then left onto Milbank Avenue.
19.6	Left onto East Elm Street.
19.9	Straight onto Davis Avenue.

20.1 Veer to the left to stay on Davis Avenue.
20.4 Right onto Indian Harbor Drive.
20.5 Right onto Museum Drive.
20.7 Back at starting point.

ings, pottery, and costumes mingle with fossils and minerals. The museum also offers monthly lectures and films and hosts a number of local associations. It is open Tuesday through Sunday and there is a small admission donation.

Stay on Museum Drive all the way to its end at Indian Harbor Drive. There, a green-and-white sign declares this to be a designated bike route. Turn left onto Indian Harbor Drive, continuing straight at the next intersection to join Davis Avenue.

Just ahead, cross a small bridge over Indian Harbor and turn left at the fork to enter **Bruce Park**, an especially beautiful public area. Ponds, walkways, playing fields, and tennis courts are found throughout for all to enjoy. A DUCK CROSSING sign warns all who pass to watch out for wandering waterfowl, which are especially prevalent in the spring when ducklings are hatched. You may wish to lean your bike against a tree and do a little wandering yourself along some of the park's paths. Our favorite leads from the road up a large rock outcropping, where flowers blossom throughout the warmer months.

At the east end of Bruce Park Drive, veer left onto Indian Field Road. Be especially cautious after crossing over the Connecticut Turnpike (Interstate 95), as the road becomes rather narrow. Cross East Putnam Avenue (Route 1) onto Old Post Road, following the latter as it hooks sharply to the right. Take the first left onto Stanwich Road for the predominantly uphill ride into northern Greenwich. Stanwich features lovely homes set on spacious estates. About a mile after joining Stanwich, stop signs mark the intersections with Indian Rock Lane and Orchard Street; the route follows Stanwich to the left in both cases. Even though Stanwich has an uphill profile overall, its scenic, wooded surroundings and light traffic make it an idyllic thoroughfare for cyclists (although it does turn bumpy for about a mile after the intersection with Dingletown Road).

At the next stop sign, leave Stanwich Road to join Guinea Road on the right for a quick side trip into Stamford. A WINDING ROAD sign ahead warns you of things to come. Amid the curves, the rutted road pavement changes as you cross into Stamford. Guinea Road is mostly downhill and heavily wooded, making this a cool run even on hot summer days. Just be careful not to build up too much speed before negotiating a pair of sharp turns ahead.

Guinea Road ends abruptly at June Road, where the route takes a sharp right-hand turn. About 0.25 mile later, cross the Mianus River and turn left onto Riverbank Road. Follow Riverbank northward to the entrance into **Riverbridge Park** on the left. Though spartan, the park provides a lovely natural setting for a midride break. Walk your bike in a ways, secure it to a tree, and continue by foot toward a small man-made waterfall. On quiet mornings all you will hear are birds singing and the brook babbling.

Retreat back onto June Road, continuing past the Guinea Road turnoff. A hard, uphill mile later, leave June Road for Tod Lane on the left. Back in Greenwich, Tod lasts only a short distance and ends at Stanwich Road. Take a right up another hill, following Stanwich to its end at Taconic Road.

Continue straight after joining Taconic. Around the bend, take a right onto South Stanwich Road. Coast down a pleasant drop toward **Rockwood Lake**, where you will have a great view of the water as you cycle over a small causeway. The scenery is magnificent all year but especially memorable in October, when autumn's colors paint the landscape.

A right turn at the end of South Stanwich puts you on North Street, beginning with a difficult uphill sprint. Thankfully, the road reverses its slope as it approaches the intersection with Lower Cross Road. Lower Cross has its ups and downs as it travels from one ridge to the next.

At the end of Lower Cross Road, turn left onto Lake Avenue to begin the trip back toward the center of town. About 0.25 mile after crossing over the Merritt Parkway (Route 15), you will come to a stop sign. Take a left onto unmarked Old Mill Road; then a quick right onto Butternut Hollow Road. Butternut begins with a welcome downward slope, followed closely by a spectacular view of **Putnam Reservoir** through the trees on the left. You will cycle past the base of the dam forming the reservoir as you turn left onto Dekraft Road just beyond the lake's southern tip.

From Dekraft climb up Dairy Road, then coast down Clapboard Ridge Road back toward North Street. In the spring, daffodils add color to the triangular island at the intersection of Clapboard Ridge and North. Adding even more color to the intersection is a **stone marker** proclaiming this to be a historic site. The monument recounts that, near this spot on December 11, 1921, an amateur radio station sent the first transatlantic message on shortwave radio (to Ardrossan, Scotland).

Continue south on North. In the spring you'll pass countless daffodils and tulips in vivid colors of yellow, white, and red. It makes you wonder where the yellow bricks are! At the end of North, bear left onto Maple Street. Maple ends quickly at the intersection with East Putnam Avenue (Route 1). On the left corner stands a **monument** to the brave soldiers of the Civil War. A Union soldier stands atop a stone pillar that is carved with the names of some of the war's more important battles. On the same small plot of land a second marker commemorates the founding of Greenwich on July 18, 1640.

Zigzagging right and then left across Route 1, continue along Milbank Avenue. A series of quick left-hand turns will take you from Milbank to East Elm Street and ultimately to Davis Avenue. After passing under the railroad and Interstate 95, bear right on Davis for the trip back to Museum Drive and your starting point.

For Further Information

Bruce Museum (203) 869–0376

Fairfield County, Connecticut

Darien

Mileage:	14
Terrain:	Moderate to rolling
Traffic:	Potentially heavy around the center of town, light elsewhere
Facilities:	Grand Union supermarket at Goodwives Shopping Center, the ride's starting point; water and rest room facilities at Pear Tree Point Beach; water fountain in the schoolyard of Darien High
Things to see:	Darien Historical Society, Washington Marker, Pear Tree Point Beach, Webb House, Rings End Landing, Stephen Mather Homestead

Although the panhandle of southwestern Connecticut continues to develop as a series of bedroom communities for Manhattan executives, the towns have never lost their countrylike charm. Darien is one such village that offers hours of pleasant cycling with minimal traffic hassles.

Begin your journey from the north exit of the Goodwives Shopping Center. There is ample parking here for those who must travel by car before departing. Bordering the shopping center to the north is the dark red colonial home of the **Darien Historical Society**. It houses a museum, which is open Thursday through Sunday afternoons. Admission is free. Both Goodwives Shopping Center and the Historical Society are located on Old Kings Highway, the first major thorough-

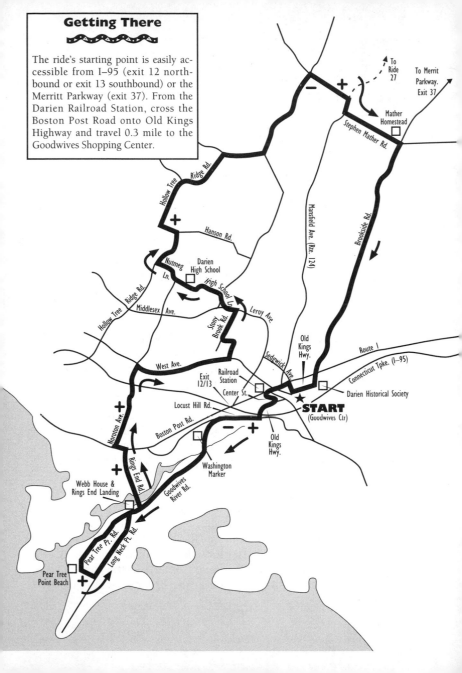

Getting There

The ride's starting point is easily accessible from I–95 (exit 12 northbound or exit 13 southbound) or the Merritt Parkway (exit 37). From the Darien Railroad Station, cross the Boston Post Road onto Old Kings Highway and travel 0.3 mile to the Goodwives Shopping Center.

To Ride 27

To Merritt Parkway. Exit 37

Mather Homestead

Stephen Mather Rd.

Ridge Rd.

Hollow Tree

Hanson Rd.

Nutmeg Ln.

Darien High School

High School Ln.

Hollow Tree Ridge Rd.

Middlesex Ave.

Stony Brook Rd.

Leroy Ave.

Mansfield Ave. (Rte. 124)

Brookside Rd.

Old Kings Hwy.

Route 1

Sedgwick Ave.

West Ave.

Connecticut Tpke. (I–95)

Exit 12/13

Railroad Station

Center St.

Darien Historical Society

Locust Hill Rd.

START
(Goodwives Ctr)

Noroton Ave.

Boston Post Rd.

Old Kings Hwy.

Washington Marker

Rings End Rd.

Goodwives River Rd.

Webb House & Rings End Landing

Pear Tree Pt. Rd.

Long Neck Pt. Rd.

Pear Tree Point Beach

DIREC-TIONS at a glance

0.0	Left out of the north exit of Goodwives Shopping Center onto Old Kings Highway.
0.1	Right at the island onto Sedgwick Avenue.
0.2	Left onto the Boston Post Road (Route 1).
0.4	Left onto Center Street.
0.5	Right onto Old Kings Highway.
0.7	Right onto Locust Hill Road.
1.2	Left onto Goodwives River Road.
2.2	Straight through stop sign and past fork.
3.3	Left onto Long Neck Point Road.
3.9	At intersection, continue to the right as Long Neck Point Road merges into Pear Tree Point Road. Just ahead, turn left onto Rings End Road.
4.5	Left onto the Boston Post Road (Route 1).
4.6	Right onto Noroton Avenue.
5.3	Right onto West Avenue.
6.1	Left onto Stony Brook Road.
6.4	Right to continue on Stony Brook Road.
6.8	At island, stay right to join Middlesex Avenue.
6.9	Left onto High School Lane.
7.1	Right through Darien High School campus, exiting through the parking lot onto Nutmeg Lane.
7.6	Right onto Hollow Tree Ridge Road.
7.8	Left to stay on Hollow Tree Ridge Road.
9.3	At stop sign, continue left around the curve.
10.2	Right onto Talmadge Hill Road.
10.6	Right onto Mansfield Avenue (Route 124).
10.7	Left onto Stephen Mather Road.
11.3	Right onto Brookside Road.
13.5	Cross intersection with Boston Post Road.
13.6	Continue straight at stop sign onto Old Kings Highway.

fare to connect colonial New York City and Boston.

Exiting the shopping center, bear left and follow the route around to the Boston Post Road (Route 1). Proceed to the left on the Post Road through the center of town *carefully!* Passing under the Metro North railroad bridge, make a left onto Center Street at the second traffic light and wind your way to Locust Hill Road, heading toward Pear Tree Point.

About 0.5 mile along Locust Hill Road, watch for a **stone marker** at the beginning of Goodwives River Road on the left. The marker proclaims that George Washington passed the point on three different occasions between 1756 and 1779, on his way to Boston. Chances are he was not on a bicycle!

Goodwives River Road follows its namesake river closely, coming to an end as the river opens to Long Island Sound. Continue straight at the stop sign, marking the end of Goodwives River Road and the beginning of Pear Tree Point Road. Looping around the point, you will pass a boat-filled marina and, next door, **Pear Tree Point Beach**. The beach is a pleasant place to stop, rest, and cool off on a warm summer day and offers a great view of Long Island.

Completing the Pear Tree Point loop on Long Neck Point Road, proceed to the left across a picturesque stone bridge over the Good-wives River. On the river's west bank is the **Webb House** (circa 1800) and **Rings End Landing**. Also known as Gorham's Landing, this was the site of one of Darien's earliest commercial centers, dating back to the early eighteenth century.

Rings End Road, an uphill run, brings you to the Boston Post Road (Route 1) and into the Noroton Heights section of Darien. Zigzag left onto Route 1, then right onto Noroton Avenue, and put on those climbing shoes once again, because it is a slow climb for the next 0.7 mile up to West Avenue. Thankfully, West Avenue is mostly level.

If you are getting a little hot about now, you will welcome the left turn onto Stony Brook Road. This heavily wooded lane can make a sweltering afternoon feel like a cool, springlike day.

At the end of Stony Brook Road, the route circles along Leroy Avenue to Middlesex Avenue, and onto High School Lane. Up ahead is

Darien High School. Take a shortcut through the school's campus to end up on Hollow Tree Ridge Road.

Now here is a road that was meant to be ridden! Hollow Tree Ridge Road will take you all the way to the New Canaan town line in style. Along the way you will pass the elegant Wee Burn Country Club, many equally elegant homes, and two stop signs. Keep to the left both times and enjoy the ride.

A third stop sign marks the northern end of both Hollow Tree Ridge Road and Darien. On the right corner of this four-way intersection is the small, quaint Talmadge Hill Community Church.

Turn right onto Talmadge Hill Road and continue to its end. Then take a right onto Mansfield Avenue (Route 124) and a left 2 blocks later onto Stephen Mather Road. Be extremely careful when turning onto Mather; there's a blind curve just ahead. (If, however, you wish to join up with Ride #27, which loops through New Canaan, turn left at Mansfield Avenue for the 2-mile ride into that town's center.)

As you approach the corner of Mather and Brookside Road (where you will turn right), take a look at the colonial house on the left corner. This is the **Stephen Mather Homestead** (circa 1778), a National Historical Landmark. Mather is best remembered as the father of the United States National Park Service. Two other Mather family homes are found farther down Brookside.

The circuit concludes as Brookside Road crosses the Boston Post Road and merges into Kings Highway. Ahead lies the Goodwives Shopping Center and your journey's end.

For Further Information

Darien Historical Society (203) 655–9233

Fairfield County, Connecticut

New Canaan

Mileage:	9
Terrain:	Rolling; hilly in spots
Traffic:	Moderate in the center of town, light elsewhere
Facilities:	Several small food stores and delis near the ride's starting point in the center of New Canaan; water and rest rooms at New Canaan Nature Center; additional food in Scotts Corners, New York, as described in the text
Things to see:	West Road colonial cemetery, New Canaan Nature Center, New Canaan Historical Society

The roads of northern New Canaan will challenge even the most seasoned cyclist. The flattest terrain is found along three north-south ridges, while east-west roads offer many ups and downs as they connect one ridge to the next. On this route you will enjoy some easier riding along all three ridges and face some truly challenging hills as you travel between them.

Leaving the center of New Canaan on Cherry Street, turn left onto Main Street as you follow the signs for Routes 124 north and 106 east. At the next intersection follow the ROUTE 106 EAST sign by turning right onto East Avenue. Don't build up too much speed going down the short hill at the beginning of East, as you must turn left almost immediately onto Forest Avenue. Follow Forest until you come

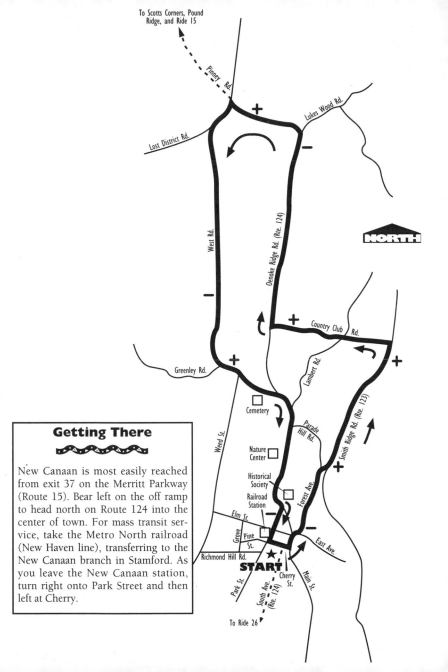

To Scotts Corners, Pound Ridge, and Ride 15

Pinney Rd.

Lost District Rd.

Lukes Wood Rd.

West Rd.

Oenoke Ridge Rd. (Rte. 124)

NORTH

Country Club Rd.

Greenley Rd.

Lambert Rd.

Smith Ridge Rd. (Rte. 123)

Cemetery

Weed St.

Getting There

New Canaan is most easily reached from exit 37 on the Merritt Parkway (Route 15). Bear left on the off ramp to head north on Route 124 into the center of town. For mass transit service, take the Metro North railroad (New Haven line), transferring to the New Canaan branch in Stamford. As you leave the New Canaan station, turn right onto Park Street and then left at Cherry.

Nature Center

Parade Hill Rd.

Historical Society

Railroad Station

Forest Ave.

Elm St.

Grove

Pine St.

East Ave.

Richmond Hill Rd.

START

Park St.

South Ave. (Rte. 124)

Cherry St.

Main St.

To Ride 26

DIREC-TIONS at a glance

0.0 Start at the intersection of South Avenue and Cherry Street; follow the signs toward Routes 124 north and 106 east.

0.1 Left onto Main Street.

0.2 Right onto East Avenue, then immediately left onto Forest Avenue.

0.6 Right, then immediately left onto Smith Ridge Road (Route 123 north).

1.8 Left onto Country Club Road.

2.7 Right onto Oenoke Ridge Road (Route 124 north).

4.2 Veer left to follow Route 124 at intersection with Lukes Woods Road. Route 124 changes names to Pinney Road.

4.8 Left onto West Road.

5.1 At stop sign, continue left on West Road.

7.5 At end of West Road, go straight to rejoin Oenoke Ridge Road (Route 124), this time heading south.

8.5 Sharp right (just before downhill) onto Park Street.

8.6 At stop sign, continue straight down hill on Park Street.

8.8 Left at second stop light onto Cherry Street.

8.9 The ride concludes at the intersection of Cherry and Main Streets.

to an island in the middle of an intersection. Turn right, then left onto Smith Ridge Road (Route 123) heading north.

An abundant shoulder makes Smith Ridge a pleasant road for cycling. As the road veers around to the left close to the crest of a fairly long hill, turn left onto Country Club Road. This is an appropriate name indeed, for the road travels along the southern edge of the New Canaan Country Club's golf course.

A few steep ups and downs later, turn to the right onto Oenoke Ridge Road (Route 124). Oenoke Ridge winds northward, alternating between shaded and open expanses. The views and scenery more than make up for the road's slow uphill slope. Keep an eye out for the New Canaan Reservoir, located below the ridge to the right along the road's long, open straightaway.

As Oenoke Ridge blends into Pinney Road around a sharp curve to the left, the terrain takes a marked turn downward toward a small bridge crossing the Rippowam River, only to be followed by an equally steep uphill run. Shortly after the hill's crest, turn left onto West Road for the return trip to New Canaan. (If all this climbing has been a bit much, and right now you want nothing more than a cold drink, continue past West Road for another mile or so. Crossing into Westchester County, New York, you will come upon a cyclist's oasis—Scotts Corners. There you will find all the amenities needed for a quick roadside refueling. Once rejuvenated, you may either pedal back up [sorry] to West Road or continue on Route 124 north into Pound Ridge. If you choose the latter, follow Rt. 124 north to Pound Ridge Road (Rt. 172). Turn left onto Pound Ridge Road, following it into the center of Bedford, where Ride #17 commences. Round trip from Scotts Corners to Bedford is 12 miles.

West Road is heavily shaded and largely downhill—just what the doctor ordered! Traveling southward, sharp-eyed cyclists will spot a small **colonial cemetery** on the right just before the intersection with Oenoke Ridge Road. Cordoned off by a wooden picket fence, the cemetery grounds are marked by a small sign that proclaims this as the first site of the Church of England in New Canaan, dating back to May 13, 1764.

Continue along Oenoke Ridge Road (Route 124) to the south. You will soon come upon the **New Canaan Nature Center** on your right. The center features hiking trails, a visitors' center, a greenhouse, a maple syrup shed, an Audubon House, and a cider mill. The immaculate grounds and trails are open daily from dawn to dusk, while the buildings are open Tuesday through Sunday. Admission is free.

As you once again approach the center of New Canaan, Oenoke Ridge Road takes a sharp turn to the left. This is your cue to prepare for an equally sharp right turn onto Park Street. Park passes between the town's green and the New Canaan Congregational Church. Across

Oenoke Ridge Road from this sharp turn is the home of the **New Canaan Historical Society.** If time permits, you might want to tour their facilities.

Continue down Park, turning to the left at the second traffic light onto Cherry Street. Follow Cherry for 1 block to the corner of South Avenue, the ride's starting point. (If you wish, turn right onto South [Route 124] and continue for 2 miles across the town line. There you may join our tour of Darien [Ride #26] at the corner of Talmadge Hill Road and Mansfield Avenue.)

For Further Information

New Canaan Historical Society (203) 966–1776
New Canaan Nature Center (203) 966–9577

28 Fairfield County, Connecticut
Fairfield Pizza Loop

Mileage:	23
Terrain:	Rolling
Traffic:	Moderate near the center of Fairfield; light elsewhere
Facilities:	Food stores near the intersection of the Post Road (Route 1) and Bulkley Road as well as on Black Rock Turn-pike *just beyond* the turn-off point onto Samp Mortar Drive; water and rest rooms in the Larson Wildlife Sanctuary as well as Southport Beach near the corner of Pequot Avenue and Sasco Creek Road
Things to see:	Ogden House, Southport Beach, Burial Hill Beach, Fairfield County Hunt Club, Hemlock Reservoir, Greenfield Hill, Bronson Windmill, Larsen Wildlife Sanctuary

Each spring, the Sound Cyclists Bicycle Club hosts the Bloomin' Metric Ride, an organized ride that attracts hundreds of the area's cyclists. Following routes that vary in length from 25 miles to 62 miles (100 kilometers or a metric century, hence the ride's name), riders climb along some of the county's finest roads, passing some magnificent estates along the way.

In addition to the Bloomin' Metric, the club holds weekend club rides throughout the year as well as several after-work rides during the summer. Each Tuesday evening during the summer months, they follow the route here, known affectionately as the Pizza Loop. The group will trace this path at a quick-paced 20 miles per hour, then gather at a local pizzeria about 2 miles to the south to eat away their pain.

The ride begins at the commuter parking lot just south of exit 44 (Black Rock Turnpike, Route 58 South) off of the Merritt Parkway. For those traveling by train, an alternate starting point might be either the Greens Farm or Southport stations, both shown on the map.

Pull out of the commuter parking lot and head south on Route 58. In about 1 mile, watch for Samp Mortar Reservoir through the trees on the right. That's a cue to turn right in about 0.2 mile onto Samp Mortar Drive. The road passes the reservoir again on the right, then crosses over Mill River, the narrow stream that flows from the reservoir to Long Island Sound. For the next 0.75 of a mile or so, the road and stream parallel one another, with a pleasant town park offering a bench or two for those who want to enjoy this small sample of nature.

The route continues straight across the intersection with Burr Street, though the road's name changes to Brookside Drive. Not far ahead, the route takes an upswing, then veers to the left onto Hill Farm Road. Another relatively small climb brings you to the end of Hill Farm, where the route turns left onto Bronson Road. Just ahead, there's a deli on the corner of Bronson and North Cedar Road if you need a quick refueling.

A little farther along Bronson, watch for Oak Lawn Cemetery on the left and the **Ogden House**, a salt-box style farmhouse built in 1750 by David Ogden, one of the area's early settlers. Run by the Fairfield Historical Society, the building is open on weekends from 1:00 to 4:00 P.M. from Mother's Day through mid-October. Tours are available.

Continue along Bronson, staying to the right at the split with Sturges Road. Not long after, you'll greet Mill River again on the left, as it makes its way toward Southport Harbor.

Pass under Interstate 95, then climb a short hill to the inter-

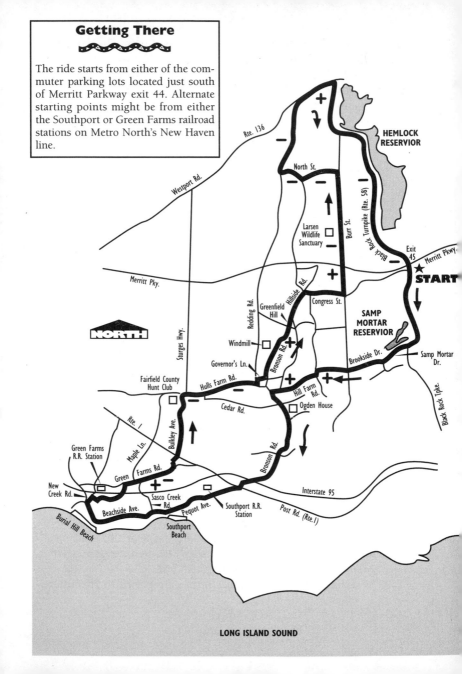

Getting There

The ride starts from either of the commuter parking lots located just south of Merritt Parkway exit 44. Alternate starting points might be from either the Southport or Green Farms railroad stations on Metro North's New Haven line.

HEMLOCK
RESERVOIR

Rte. 136

Westport Rd.

North St.

Larsen
Wildlife
Sanctuary

Merritt Pky.

Burr St.

Black Rock Turnpike (Rte. 58)

Exit
45

Merritt Pkwy.

START

Congress St.

SAMP
MORTAR
RESERVIOR

Redding Rd.

Hillside Rd.

Greenfield
Hill

Windmill

Brookside Dr.

Samp Mortar
Dr.

Sturges Hwy.

NORTH

Governor's Ln.

Bronson Rd.

Hill Farm
Rd.

Fairfield County
Hunt Club

Hulls Farm Rd.

Cedar Rd.

Ogden House

Black Rock Tpke.

Bulkley Ave.

Rte. 1

Maple Ln.

Green Farms
R.R. Station

Bronson Rd.

Green Farms Rd.

Interstate 95

New
Creek Rd.

Beachside Ave.

Sasco Creek
Rd.

Pequot Ave.

Southport R.R.
Station

Post Rd. (Rte.1)

Burial Hill Beach

Southport
Beach

LONG ISLAND SOUND

DIREC-TIONS at a glance

0.0 Start at Commuter Car Pool Lot at Merritt Parkway exit 44. Turn onto Route 58 heading south (away from the Merritt).
1.2 Turn right onto Samp Mortar Drive.
2.2 Continue straight on Brookside Drive.
2.5 Veer to the left onto Hill Farm Road.
3.5 Turn left onto Bronson Road.
5.5 Turn left onto Mill Hill Road.
5.6 Turn right onto Pequot Avenue.
7.1 Bear left onto Beachside Avenue.
8.3 Turn right onto New Creek Road.
8.5 Turn right onto Maple Lane.
9.1 Make a right onto Green Farms Road.
10.0 Bear left onto Bulkley Avenue.
11.3 Turn right onto Hulls Farm Road.
12.4 Turn left onto Redding Road.
12.5 Turn right onto Governors Lane.
12.6 Bear left onto Bronson Avenue.
13.6 Turn left onto Hillside Road.
14.1 Take a right onto Congress Street.
14.8 Turn left onto Burr Street.
16.8 Make a left onto North Street.
17.9 Turn right onto Redding Road.
19.0 Bear right onto Westport Road (Route 136).
19.6 Turn right onto Black Rock Turnpike (Route 58).
23.2 Turn right into the Commuter Parking Lot.

section with Mill Hill Road. Follow the sign To U.S. 1 to the left, crossing over the railroad tracks, then turn right onto Pequot Avenue, passing under the Boston Post Road (Route 1) and continuing into the center of Southport. Exiting the town, you will pass many magnificent estates along this tree-lined road, along with the Southport Congregational Church, a magnificent stone gothic church. A little ways down the road lies Long Island Sound and **Southport Beach**. If the day is hot, this is the perfect place to stop and cool off for a while.

Crossing over Sasco Creek, the road's name changes to Beachside Avenue as it enters the neighboring town of Westport. Ahead, as the road loops to the right, lies **Burial Hill Beach**. Follow the road as it merges into New Creek Road, then just ahead, turn right onto Maple Lane to continue the route. Soon after passing under the railroad tracks and Interstate 95, Maple intersects Greens Farms Road, where the route turns right. Climb a long, low hill up Greens Farms, then enjoy the coast down as you approach the left turn onto Bulkley Avenue. Just 0.2 mile down Bulkley brings you to the Boston Post Road (Route 1). This is a confusing intersection, as to stay on Bulkley, you'll have to cross diagonally to the right, then left. Please wait for the traffic light, and then proceed with caution.

Continue along Bulkley all the way to its end at Hulls Farm Road. Just before that T intersection, watch for the **Fairfield County Hunt Club** on the left. You may want to pause here for a moment to watch riders put horses through their paces. A right onto Hulls Farm Road carries you over Sasco Creek once again and back into Fairfield. The town greets you with another upward climb, topping off about 0.3 mile later, followed by a refreshing downhill descent.

Keep an eye out for a red barn on the left, for that is your cue to turn left onto Redding Road. The route doesn't stay on Redding for long, for it's another quick right onto Governor's Lane, then an equally quick left onto Bronson Road. Continue along Bronson, up a hill, until you come to the **Frederick Bronson Windmill** about 0.5 mile down on the left. The windmill was erected in 1890 and restored by concerned citizens in 1974. Perched atop the tall, brown tower is a massive copper weathervane turned green with age.

Not far past the Bronson Windmill lies **Greenfield Hill**, the quintessential New England setting. Surrounded by a multitude of dogwood trees is the picturesque Greenfield Congregational

Church. Each spring, a Dogwood Festival is held here to celebrate the trees' blossoming. It's a lovely event not to be missed.

After Greenfield Hill, veer to the right to stay on Bronson, then just ahead, turn left onto Hillside Road. Ride 0.5 mile and then turn right onto unmarked Congress Street, then another 0.5 mile or so later, turn left onto Burr Street. Burr begins with a climb as it heads up and over the Merritt Parkway, followed by a quick descent on the other side. Though it's tempting to build up speed, be sure to slow down in time to turn into the **Larsen Wildlife Sanctuary** down the hill on the left. The Larsen Sanctuary, operated by the Connecticut Audubon Society, is a 160-acre wildlife refuge that features 6 miles of boardwalk trails through the woods. The recently remodeled visitors' center features exhibits, a lecture hall, reference library, and a well-stocked nature store. The sanctuary is open daily from dawn to dusk, while the nature center is open Tuesday through Saturday from 9:00 A.M. to 4:30 P.M., as well as Sundays from noon to 4:30 P.M. except in January, February, July, and August. There is a small admission charge.

Continue north on Burr Street to the four-way intersection with North Street, where the route turns left. North Street is a wild and wooly ride that heads straight down after a brief uphill slope in the beginning. Be sure to hold on tight, as the road is narrow, winding, and very definitely downhill. At its end, turn right onto Redding Road, heading north into Easton. Take a right onto Westport Road (Route 136), then 0.5 mile later, right again onto Black Rock Turnpike (Route 58), to head south back into Fairfield.

As the road slopes primarily downhill back to the ride's beginning, be sure to enjoy the magnificent view of **Hemlock Reservoir** on the left. The scenery is especially beautiful in the autumn when the trees surrounding the reservoir paint the landscape with fiery colors of orange, yellow, and red. Finally, passing the reservoir's dam, the road takes a noticeable dip down for a quick return to the Merritt Parkway and the commuter parking lot where the ride began. Anyone for some pizza?

For Further Information

Ogden House (203) 259–1598
Larsen Wildlife Sanctuary (203) 259–6305

Morris/Sussex Counties, New Jersey
Lake Hopatcong

Mileage:	16
Terrain:	Hilly
Traffic:	Light to moderate
Facilities:	Water and rest rooms at the marinas along Espanong Road, just before Brady Road, as well as in Hopatcong State Park; food supplies available from several stores along the route, including the shopping center at the ride's starting point, as well as markets along Espanong Road and River Styx Road (near Lakeside Blvd.)
Things to see:	Lake Hopatcong, Hopatcong State Park

Northwestern New Jersey, nicknamed the Skylands, offers some of the finest (and hilliest) cycling terrain in the tristate region. Dominating the area is the state's largest body of water, **Lake Hopatcong.** Actually, when Europeans first settled the area in the early 1700s, they found here not one, but rather two, bodies of water. The smaller, northern lake was christened Little Pond, while the larger was named Great Pond or Brooklyn Pond. They were connected by the Musconetcong River.

With the discovery of iron ore in the 1750s, the region quickly developed a strong mining industry. The Brooklyn Forge, built along the Musconetcong between the lakes, supplied Washington's troops stationed in Moorestown during the American Revolution.

173

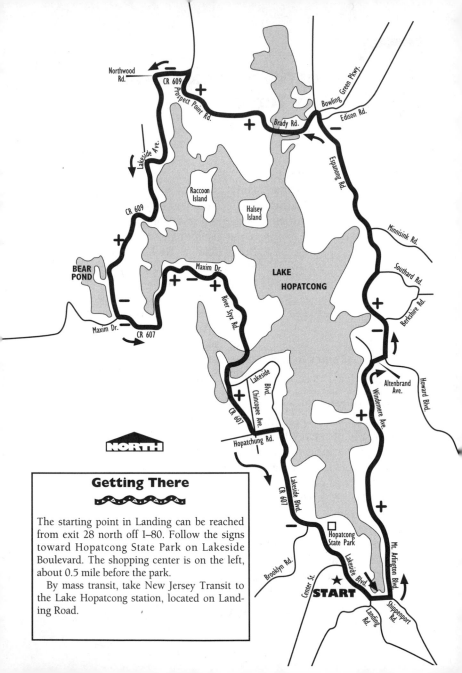

NORTH

Getting There

The starting point in Landing can be reached from exit 28 north off I–80. Follow the signs toward Hopatcong State Park on Lakeside Boulevard. The shopping center is on the left, about 0.5 mile before the park.

By mass transit, take New Jersey Transit to the Lake Hopatcong station, located on Landing Road.

DIREC-TIONS at a glance	0.0 Head east on Lakeside Boulevard from Grand Union Shopping Center.
	0.4 Left at traffic light onto unmarked Shippenport Road.
	0.5 Left onto Mount Arlington Boulevard.
	2.8 Follow road toward the right onto Altenbrand Avenue.

3.0 Left onto Howard Boulevard.

5.8 Left onto Brady Road.

7.5 Left onto Northwood Road (County Route 609).

10.3 Left onto Maxim Drive (County Route 607).

13.6 Left at stop sign onto Hopatchung Road.

13.8 Right onto Lakeside Boulevard.

15.7 Right into shopping center.

As the mining industry began to ebb because of the high cost of shipping the ore, the forge was dismantled and replaced by a dam. Completed in 1827, the dam raised the water in the river valley to form one large lake. The newly formed lake was named Hopatcong, from the Indian word *Huppakong,* meaning "honey waters of many coves."

Subsequently, a canal was built to link the lake with Easton, Pennsylvania to the west and Jersey City, New Jersey to the east. It took five days for mule-drawn barges to make the trip; they were soon replaced by the locomotive. The canal was abandoned and the lake returned to its natural serenity.

On this ride, you will experience firsthand the serenity of Lake Hopatcong while encountering the challenges of Morris and Sussex counties' countryside. Begin at the Grand Union Shopping Center at the corner of Lakeside Boulevard and Center Street in Landing. Though it is always a good idea to bring from home everything you will need on a ride, it's nice to know that the shopping center features a grocery store, a deli, and a bike shop . . . just in case!

With your needs and those of your trusty steed now satisfied, push eastward on Lakeside. Just down the road, after catching your first glimpse of the lake, turn left at the traffic light onto unmarked Shippenport Road. A second left onto Mount Arlington Boulevard aims you northward along the eastern shore of Hopatcong. Though the road starts out bumpy and narrow, it improves in about a mile as it crosses into Mount Arlington. All along, watch as the houses on the left begin to sink below the grade of the road. The steeply inclined bank affords you a good view of their roofs and an even better glimpse of the water.

Follow the road to the right as it veers into Altenbrand Avenue. Just ahead a left at the stop sign puts you on Howard Boulevard. Enjoy the brief downhill respite as Howard dives toward the lake's Van Every Cove, where you will find a marina, boat rentals, and another great lakeside panorama.

A few more ups and downs later, turn left onto Brady Road. It would be very easy to ride right by this turn without ever noticing it, were it not for the sign—not the street sign but the sign across the way advertising CHABON'S BAR. You can't miss it.

Brady Road begins with a flat stretch until it crosses Brady Bridge; then it's upward once again. As the hill tops out at Schwarz Road, Brady's name changes to Prospect Point Road. Incidentally, you may think you have wandered into Washington, D.C., after the bridge, as you cycle past avenues with states' names.

Turn left onto Northwood Road (County Route 609) and cross into Sussex County. Bordered by few houses, Northwood winds through thick woodlands, up some hills, and down others and is a great road for cycling. As it ends at Maxim Drive (County Route 607) you can sneak a peek at Bear Pond on the right if you want, but the ride proceeds along River Styx Road to the left for the (mostly) downhill trip through the borough of Hopatcong. Continue across the bridge over River Styx to the road's end at a stop sign. Turn left onto Hopatchung Road, then right up ahead onto Lakeside Boulevard.

For the final leg of the journey, Lakeside Boulevard obliges with a downhill profile. Close to the bottom of the hill lies **Hopatcong State Park** on the left. A small admission fee is charged. The park features a swimming beach, picnic area, fishing, and a refreshment stand. A museum, run by the local historical society, is open to visitors daily from 1:00 to 4:00 P.M. Why not ride the half mile back to the shopping center, pick up some food, and return to the park for an end-of-the-ride picnic? Go ahead, you deserve it.

For Further Information

Lake Hopatcong (973) 770–1200
Hopatcong State Park (973) 398–7010

Bergen County, New Jersey
Harrington Park and Vicinity

Mileage:	14
Terrain:	Mostly flat
Traffic:	Light to moderate
Facilities:	Rest rooms and water available in the Harrington Park Library, Pascack Brook County Park, and River Vale Public Library (on River Vale Road, near Sunset Road); food available from a number of delis and food stores near the intersection of Oradell Avenue and Kinderkamack Road as well as at the intersections of Old Hook Road and River Vale Road
Things to see:	Abram Demaree Homestead, Oradell Reservoir, Lafayette marker, Pascack Brook County Park, Baylor's Massacre site, Lake Tappan, Pondside Park

We have always liked this town in northern Bergen County, New Jersey. Its name has such a pleasant ring to it! (Of course, we Harringtons might be a little biased in its favor.) On this ride you will pass through Harrington Park as well as a number of other "bedroom communities" to New York City.

Begin at the Harrington Park Public Library and Municipal Center on Harriot Avenue. Turn left out of the parking lot. At the corner of Harriot, Tappan Road, and Schraalenburgh Road, turn right, heading south on the latter. Be sure to stay to the right as Closter Road forks to the left. Shortly, at the edge of town, Schraalenburgh passes over a small stream called Dwarskill.

On the right corner of the intersection of Old Hook Road, take a few minutes to visit the **Abram Demaree Homestead**. Demaree, a farmer from Holland, purchased the house, barn, and adjacent land here in 1769. (The house dates back to 1720; the barn to the late 1600s.) Today Demaree's home has been transformed into an old-fashioned country store featuring more than one million crafts, gifts, and seasonal decorations. Hours vary by season, so be sure to phone ahead.

Continue down Schraalenburgh until the junction with Durie Avenue, where the ride turns right. A little way down the road, just before the railroad crossing, Durie shoots off to the left, but you should continue straight onto Lake Shore Drive. Not far down Lake Shore, a sign suddenly proclaims that the road ends ahead, forcing you to take a left onto Maple Street. Now in the town of Haworth, the ride along Maple leads through a lovely, shady neighborhood of pleasant homes.

Maple ends at the juncture with Sunset Avenue. A right turn here takes you on a course straight toward White Beeches Country Club and **Oradell Reservoir**. In fact, the road slices through the club's property, affording a good view of the well-manicured golf course.

At the end of Sunset Avenue, with the reservoir dead ahead, keep to the left as the road becomes Grant Avenue. Follow the green-and-white BIKE ROUTE signs to the right onto First Street for a quick jaunt through another quiet neighborhood.

At the street's end turn right onto Oradell Avenue for the trip into its namesake village. Just after crossing the Oradell Veterans Memorial Bridge over the tip of the reservoir, you will pass a small park on the right. A stone marker in the center proclaims this to be a memorial to veterans of World War I.

Turn right onto Kinderkamack Road (County Route 51). Kinderkamack can be a busy thoroughfare at times, so ride with caution. Be especially wary of cars parked along the road whose drivers suddenly open their doors into traffic.

About 0.5 mile later, on the left-hand side of Kinderkamack, is a historical **marker** situated in front of a high ridge. The sign notes that

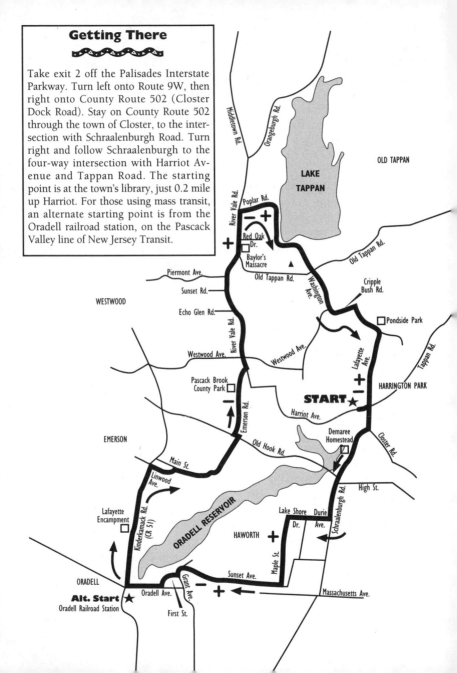

Getting There

Take exit 2 off the Palisades Interstate Parkway. Turn left onto Route 9W, then right onto County Route 502 (Closter Dock Road). Stay on County Route 502 through the town of Closter, to the intersection with Schraalenburgh Road. Turn right and follow Schraalenburgh to the four-way intersection with Harriot Avenue and Tappan Road. The starting point is at the town's library, just 0.2 mile up Harriot. For those using mass transit, an alternate starting point is from the Oradell railroad station, on the Pascack Valley line of New Jersey Transit.

OLD TAPPAN

LAKE TAPPAN

Middletown Pd.

Orangeburgh Rd.

River Vale Rd.

Poplar Rd.

Red Oak Dr.

Baylor's Massacre

Old Tappan Rd.

Old Tappan Rd.

Washington Ave.

Cripple Bush Rd.

Pondside Park

Tappan Rd.

Piermont Ave.

Sunset Rd.

WESTWOOD

Echo Glen Rd.

River Vale Rd.

Westwood Ave.

Westwood Ave.

Lafayette Ave.

HARRINGTON PARK

Pascack Brook County Park

START

Harriot Ave.

Emerson Rd.

EMERSON

Old Hook Rd.

Demaree Homestead

Closter Rd.

Main St.

Linwood Ave.

High St.

Lafayette Encampment

Kinderkamack Rd. (CR 51)

ORADELL RESERVOIR

Lake Shore Dr.

Durie Ave.

HAWORTH

Schraalenburgh Rd.

Maple St.

ORADELL

Alt. Start
Oradell Railroad Station

Oradell Ave.

Grant Ave.

First St.

Sunset Ave.

Massachusetts Ave.

DIREC-TIONS at a glance

0.0 Begin at Harrington Park Library on Harriot Avenue.
0.2 Right onto Schraalenburgh Road.
0.4 Right to stay on Schraalenburgh Road.
1.6 Right onto Durie Avenue.
1.7 Straight onto Lake Shore Drive.
2.1 Left onto Maple Street.
2.9 Right onto Sunset Avenue.
4.2 Left onto Grant Avenue.
4.4 Right onto First Street.
4.7 Right onto Oradell Avenue.
5.1 Right onto Kinderkamack Road (County Route 51).
6.6 Right onto Linwood Avenue (merges ahead into Main Street).
8.1 Left onto Old Hook Road.
8.2 Right onto Emerson Road.
8.9 Left onto River Vale Road.
10.3 Left to stay on River Vale Road.
11.0 Right onto Poplar Road.
12.4 Straight across Old Tappan Road onto Washington Avenue.
12.9 Follow road to left onto Cripple Bush Road.
13.3 Right onto Blanch Avenue.
13.7 Right onto Lafayette Road.
14.5 Right onto Harriot Avenue.
14.9 Back at starting point.

for about two weeks in September 1778, the French general Lafayette chose this ridge as a campsite for the Continental Army. Today the army tents of two centuries ago have been replaced by three contemporary homes.

Just after crossing the railroad tracks at the Emerson train station, turn right onto Linwood Avenue and continue onto Main Street. When Main Street ends at Old Hook Road, take a left followed by an immediate right onto Emerson Road. Before the road crosses into the town of River Vale, you will pass **Pascack Brook County Park** on the left. This is a great place to pull over for a midride reprieve.

At the next major intersection, turn left onto River Vale Road. As you approach Echo Glen Road on the left, a bike-route sign points to the start of a paved bicycle path, also on the left. Though the path is wonderful while it lasts, it ends in about 0.5 mile at Sunset Road.

As Old Tappan Road joins in from the right, a brown-and-white sign straight ahead marks the site of **Baylor's Massacre**. Take a quick right onto Red Oak Drive to enter the commemorative park. The sign there reads: IN MEMORIAL OF AMERICAN SOLDIERS KILLED DURING THE REVOLUTIONARY WAR IN THE BAYLOR MASSACRE ON SEPTEMBER 28, 1778. LIEUTENANT COLONEL GEORGE BAYLOR'S THIRD REGIMENT OF CONTINENTAL DRAGOONS TOOK QUARTERS FOR THE NIGHT AT SEVERAL NEARBY FARMS. TORIES BETRAYED THEIR PRESENCE TO A BRITISH FORCE, WHO SURROUNDED THE DRAGOONS DURING THE NIGHT. A NUMBER OF AMERICANS WERE KILLED OR WOUNDED AFTER THEY HAD SURRENDERED. The park features paved footpaths that wander through the woods toward the Hackensack River.

Turn right onto Poplar Road and enjoy a brief downhill run. But, remembering one of our laws of bicycling ("whatever goes down must go up"), get ready to pedal back up toward the shore of **Lake Tappan**. What a lovely ride this is along the lake's southwest shore! The view is especially breathtaking during autumn. You will soon cross a small bridge adjacent to the dam that regulates the water's depth. The prominent green pipe spanning the dam's width seems to be a favorite hangout for the local seagulls!

Leaving the lake behind, the road's name changes to Washington Avenue. Continue across Old Tappan Road, veering to the left at its end onto Cripple Bush Road. A short while later take a right onto Blanch Avenue, where a sign welcomes you back into Harrington Park. Although the ride turns right onto Lafayette Street, you may first elect to stop at **Pondside Park** on the left. The park, which features benches and a popular playground, is dedicated to the town's volunteers who "enrich Harrington Park life." It's a short trip down Lafayette to Harriot, then a right to the ride's point of departure.

For Further Information

Abram Demaree Homestead (201) 784–9618

Appendix I
Bicycle Shops and Rental Centers

Here is a brief list of some of the many fine bicycle shops and rental centers found in the tristate area. This list is by no means exhaustive, nor does it imply any endorsement by the authors or publisher.

Manhattan

Bicycle Habitat, 244 Lafayette Street; (212) 431–3315

Bicycle Renaissance, 430 Columbus Avenue; (212) 724–2350

Canal Street Bicycles, 417 Canal Street; (212) 334–8000

Eddie's Bicycle Shop, 490 Amsterdam Avenue; (212) 580–2011

Frank's Bike Shop, 553 Grand Street; (212) 533–6332

Loeb Boathouse, East Park Drive, Central Park; (212) 288–7281

Metro Bicycles, 231 West 96th Street; (212) 663–7531

Brooklyn

Bay Ridge Bicycle World, 8916 3rd Avenue; (718) 238–1118

Bicycle Land, 424 Coney Island Avenue; (718) 633–0820

Brooklyn Bicycle Center, 715 Coney Island Avenue; (718) 941–9095

City Line Bicycle Center, 1201 Liberty Avenue; (718) 647–2501

Larry's Cycle Shop, 1854 Flatbush Avenue; (718) 377–3600

P & H Bicycle Store, 1819 Coney Island Avenue; (718) 998–4333

Roy's Sheepshead Cycle, 2679 Coney Island Avenue; (718) 646–9430

Sizzling Bicycle, Inc., 3100 Ocean Parkway; (718) 372–8985

Queens

Bicycle Barn, 10734 Springfield Boulevard, Queens Village; (718) 479–3119

Bicycle Place, 45-70 Kissena Boulevard, Flushing; (718) 358–0986

Bicycles in Flushing Meadow Park; (718) 669–9598

Buddy's Schwinn Bicycles, 79-30 Parsons Boulevard, Flushing; (718) 591–9180

Century Bicycle Shop, 1418 150th Street, Flushing; (718) 767–2772

Kantor's Bicycle Rental & Sales, 9415 100th Street, Ozone Park; (718) 322–2222

Roberts Bicycle, 33-13 Francis Lewis Boulevard, Bayside; (718) 353–5432

Bronx

Arrow Cycle Inc., 4053 White Plains Road; (718) 547–2656

Bronx Bike Center, 912 East Gun Hill Road; (718) 798–3242

Burke's Bicycle Shop, 941 Intervale Avenue; (718) 328–9197

Castle Hill Bicycle Center, 1010 Castle Hill Avenue; (718) 597–2083

Crosstown Bicycle, 33 East 170th Street; (718) 293–8837

Eddie's Cycle Center, 2035 Grand Concourse; (718) 731–0322

Kantor's Bicycle Store, 3395 White Plains Road; (718) 583–1030

Sid's Bike Shop, 215 West 230th Street; (718) 549–8247

Westchester Bicycle Pro Shop, 2611 Westchester Avenue; (718) 409–1114

Staten Island

Bennett's Bicycles, 517 Jewett Avenue; (718) 447–8652

Bicycle Medic, 796 Castleton Avenue; (718) 442–5800

Bike Shop of Staten Island, 4026 Hylan Boulevard; (718) 948–4184

John's Schwinn Bicycle Shop, 1764 Victory Boulevard; (718) 981–1691

Nassau County, Long Island

Bike Junkies, 323 Broadway, Bethpage; (516) 932–7271

Bikeworks, 7 Northern Boulevard, Greenvale; (516) 484–4422

Brand's Cycle Center, 1966 Wantagh Avenue, Wantagh; (516) 781–6100

Danny's Ride-A-Way, 3259 Hempstead Turnpike, Levittown; (516) 579–7770

Family Bicycle Shop, 3801 Hempstead Turnpike, Levittown; (516) 735–1010

Sunrise Cyclery, 4828 Sunrise Highway, Massapequa Park; (516) 798–-5715

Suffolk County, Long Island

Cycle Company, 564 Jericho Turnpike, Smithtown; (516) 979–7078

Frenchie's Cycle World, 165 Walt Whitman Road, Huntington Station; (516) 673–6002

Smithtown Bicycle and Fitness Center, 11 West Main Street, Smithtown; (516) 265–5900

Spokehouse Cycle, 675 East Jericho Turnpike, Huntington Station; (516) 385–0808

Westchester County, New York

A-1 Bicycle Repair Service, 12 Concord Drive, Peekskill; (914) 528–7438

American Cycle, 1770 Crompond Road, Peekskill; (914) 739–7533

Bicycle Express, 52 Virginia Road, North White Plains; (914) 428–2305

Bicycle Righter, 119 Cedar Road, Katonah; (914) 232–4875

Bicycle World, 141 Main Street, Mount Kisco; (914) 666–4044

Big Cycle, 9 Norm Avenue, Bedford Hills; (914) 666–3549

Hickory and Tweed Ski & Cycle, 410 Main Street, Armonk; (914) 273–3397

High Caliper Bicycle Company, 169 Mamaroneck Avenue, White Plains; (914) 683–5603

Miller's Bikes, 335 Mamaroneck Avenue, Mamaroneck; (914) 698–5070

Paulding's Cycle Store, 98 West Post Road, White Plains; (914) 949–5527

Rye Bike Shop, 30 Elm Place, Rye; (914) 967–2849

Putnam County, New York

Village Bikes, 88 North Main Street, Brewster; (914) 279–9689

Wheel & Heel Limited, 65 Gleneida Avenue, Carmel; (914) 228–1206

Rockland County, New York

Congers Bike Shop, 107 Lake Road, Congers; (914) 268–3315

Nyack Bicycle Outfitters, 72 North Broadway, Nyack; (914) 353–0268

Valley Cycle, 139 East Route 59, Spring Valley; (914) 356–3179

Orange County, New York

Barry's Bikes, 1 Oakland Avenue, Warwick; (914) 987–1614

Bicycle Doctor, 30 East Main Street, Middletown; (914) 344–1414

Mark's Cycle Corner, 154 Wickham Avenue, Middletown; (914) 343–4480

Oake's Cycle Shop, Route 17 M, Monroe; (914) 783–2585

Fairfield County, Connecticut

Buzz's Cycle Shop, Post Road, Old Greenwich; (203) 637–1665

Cycle Dynamics, Riversville Road, Greenwich; (203) 532–1718

Don's Cycle Shop, 1964 Post Road, Fairfield; (203) 255–4079

Greenwich Bicycles, 40 West Putnam Avenue, Greenwich; (203) 869–4141

New Canaan Cyclery, 94 Park Street, New Canaan; (203) 966–2399

Pedal and Pump, 51 Tokeneke Road, Darien; (203) 655–2600

Westport Bicycles, 1252 Post Road East, Westport; (203) 222–1998

Bergen County, New Jersey

Albert's Westwood Cycle, 182 Third Avenue, Westwood; (201) 664–1688

Paramus Cycle, 23 Farview Place, Paramus; (201) 368–8242

Morris County, New Jersey

Bicycle Outlet, State Highway 15, Lake Hopatcong; (201) 663–1935

Treasure Town Cycle Cyclery, 175 Lakeside Boulevard, Landing; (201) 398–9030

Appendix II

Bicycle Clubs in and around New York City

National

Adventure Cycling, P.O. Box 8308, Missoula, MO 59807; adv-cycling.org

League of American Bicyclists, 190 West Ostende Street, Suite 120, Baltimore, MD 21230; www.bikeleague.org

New York

American Youth Hostels/Hostelling International, New York Council, 891 Amsterdam Avenue, New York, NY 10025; www.hostelling.com

Century Road Club Association, P.O. Box 20412, Greeley Square Station, NY 10001; www.cc.columbia.edu/~adr5/crca.html

Concerned Long Island Mountain Bicyclists (C.L.I.M.B.), P.O. Box 203, Woodbury, NY 11797; www.bicyclelongisland.org/climb.htm

Country Cycle Club, Inc., 1 Willowbrook Road, White Plains, NY 10605

Five Borough Bicycle Club, 891 Amsterdam Avenue, New York, NY 10025; www.panix.com/~fivebbc

German Bicycle Sports Club, 298 Bayville Avenue, Bayville, NY 11709; www.intercall.com/~ips/gbsc/gbsc.htm

Huntington Bicycle Club, P.O. Box 322, Huntington Station, NY 11746; www.bicyclelongisland.org/hbc.htm

Long Island Bicycle Club, 73-18 180th Street, Flushing, NY 11366; www.intercall.com/~ips/libc/libc.htm

Massapequa Park Bicycle Club, 219 North 3rd Street, Bethpage, NY 11714; www.li.net/~msmingel/mpbc.html

Mid-Hudson Bicycle Club, P.O. Box 1727, Poughkeepsie, NY 12601; www.hvn.net/~mhbc

New York Cycle Club, P.O. Box 20541, Columbus Circle Station, New York, NY 10023; www.nycc.org

Orange County Bicycle Club, 48 South Street, Warwick, NY 10916; www.sussexonline.com/ocbc

Paumonauk Bicycle Clubs, Inc., P.O. Box 7159A, Hicksville, NY 11802; www.bicyclelongisland.org

Sleepy Hollow Bicycle Club, 95 Beekman Avenue, North Tarrytown, NY 10591; www.shbc.org/shbc/home.html

Staten Island Bicycling Association, P.O. Box 141016, Staten Island, NY 10314; www.bike.princeton.edu/siba

Suffolk Bicycle Riders Association, P.O. Box 544, Nesconset, NY 11767; www.bicyclelongisland.org/sbra.htm

Transportation Alternatives (bicycling advocacy organization), 494 Broadway, New York, NY 10012; www.transalt.org

Connecticut
Central Connecticut Cycling, 27 Lillian Drive; Trumbull, CT 06611

Hat City Cyclists, 11 Elm Street, #2, Norwalk, CT 06850; gaboon.imcinternet.net/hcc.html

Sound Cyclists Bicycle Club, 66 Overlook Road, Fairfield, CT 06430; www.soundcyclists.com

New Jersey
Bicycling Touring Club of North Jersey, P.O. Box 839, Mahwah, NJ 07430; home.att.net/~btcnj

Central Jersey Bicycle Club, P.O. Box 2202, Edison, NJ 08818; turbo.kean.edu/~kbowker/cjbc/cjbcmems.html

Jersey Shore Touring Society, P.O. Box 8581, Red Bank, NJ 07701; www.erols.com/jsts

Morris Area Freewheelers, P.O. Box 331, Lake Hiawatha, NJ 07034; users.aol.com/atbbiker/fwnews/mafinfo.html

North Jersey Bicycle Club, 100 Ridgewald Avenue, Waldwick, NJ 07463

Outdoor Club of New Jersey P.O. Box 1508, Riverside, NJ 08075

Princeton Freewheelers, Inc., P.O. Box 1204, Princeton, NJ 08542; www.bike.princeton.edu/pfw

Ridgewood Cycle Club, Inc., 35 North Broad Street, Ridgewood, NJ 07450

Shore Cycle Club, P.O. Box 492, Northfield, NJ 08225

Sussex County Touring Club, 17 North Orchard Terrace, Sparta, NJ 07871

Western Jersey Wheelmen, P.O. Box 230-B, Philhower Road, Lebanon, NJ 08833; www.bike.princeton.edu/wjw

Appendix III

Annual Cycling Events in and around New York City

All area bicycle clubs hold regular group rides for their members, but many also sponsor large rides that attract hundreds, even thousands, of cyclists from around the tristate area. All of the rides below are open to the public, although most require a registration fee. For that, you get a cue sheet and map, food stops, and "SAG support" (a car that picks up you and your bike in case one of you can't finish the ride). Send a self-addressed, stamped envelope to the sponsoring club for further information. (See Appendix II for bike club addresses.)

New York

Bike-Boat-Bike Ride, sponsored by Suffolk Bike Riders Association
Five Boro Bicycle Tour, sponsored by American Youth Hostels
Gold Coast Tour, sponsored by Huntington Bicycle Club
Golden Apple Century, sponsored by Country Cycle Club
High Point Hundred, sponsored by Paumonauk Bicycle Clubs
New York City Century Ride-A-Thon, sponsored by Transportation Alternatives
New York Ride Across the State, sponsored by Mid-Hudson Bicycle Club
Orange County Country Roads Tour, sponsored by Orange County Bicycle Club

Connecticut

Bloomin' Metric Century, sponsored by Sound Cyclists Bicycle Club
Hat City Cyclefest, sponsored by Hat City Cyclists

New Jersey

Hillier Than Thou Century, sponsored by Central Jersey Bicycle
    Club

Jersey Double, sponsored by Western Jersey Wheelmen

New Jersey Farmlands Flat Tour, sponsored by Central Jersey
    Bicycle Club

Pinelands Metric Century, sponsored by Shore Cycle Club

Princeton Bicycling Event, sponsored by Princeton Freewheelers

Raritan Valley Round-Up, sponsored by Central Jersey Bicycle Club

Appendix IV

Off-Road Riding in and around New York City

Although this book is geared toward road riding, the New York tri-state area has many wonderful areas for off-road and trail cycling. Here is a list of trails scattered throughout the region that you might enjoy exploring on a mountain bike or hybrid, along with addresses and phone numbers for further information. Be sure to check if there are any permits required or other restrictions before venturing out on the trails.

One request: Whenever riding off-road, please remember to follow the "Rules of the Trail" offered by the International Mountain Biking Association:

1. Ride on open trails only.
2. Leave no trace.
3. Control your bicycle.
4. Always yield trail to hikers and walkers.
5. Never scare wild animals.
6. Plan ahead.

Nassau/Suffolk Counties, Long Island, New York
Bethpage State Park, Farmingdale
Bethpage State Park
Farmingdale, NY 11735
(516) 249–0701

Caumsett State Park, Huntington
Caumsett State Park
West Neck Road
Huntington, NY 11743
(516) 423–1770

Fire Island National Seashore, Fire Island
National Park Service
120 Laurel Street
Patchogue, NY 11772
(516) 289–4810

Nassau-Suffolk Greenbelt, Woodbury
Long Island Greenbelt Conference
23 Deer Path Road
Central Islip, NY 11722
(516) 360–0753

Stillwell Woods County Park, Syosset
Long Island Greenbelt Conference
23 Deer Path Road
Central Islip, NY 11722
(516) 360–0753

Rockland County, New York
Harriman State Park, Bear Mountain
Palisades Interstate Park Commission
Bear Mountain, NY 10911
(914) 786–2701

Raymond G. Esposito Trail, South Nyack
Village of South Nyack
282 South Broadway
South Nyack, NY 10960
(914) 358–0287

Orange County, New York
Orange Heritage Trail, Goshen to Mouroe
Orange County Dept. of Parks, Recreation & Conservation
550 Route 416
Montgomery, NY 12549
(914) 457–4900

Putnam County, New York
Clarence Fahnestock State Park, Carmel
Clarence Fahnestock State Park
RFD 2
Carmel, NY 10512
(914) 225–7207

Westchester County, New York
Blue Mountain Reservation, Peekskill
Blue Mountain Reservation
Welcher Avenue
Peekskill, NY 10566
(914) 593–7275

Franklin D. Roosevelt State Park, Yorktown Heights
Franklin D. Roosevelt State Park
2965 Crompond Road
Yorktown Heights, NY 10598
(914) 245–4434

Graham Hills Park, Pleasantville
Graham Hills Park
Route 117
Pleasantville, NY 10570
(914) 232–4905

North County Trailway, Mount Pleasant
Westchester County Parks & Recreation
25 Moore Ave #1-2
Mount Kisco, NY 10549
(914) 242–6300

Old Croton Aqueduct Trail, Croton-On-Hudson (trail goes from
New Croton Reservoir all the way to the Bronx-Yonkers border)
Taconic State Park Commission
Old Post Road
Staatsburg, NY 12580
(914) 889–4100

Connecticut
Collis P. Huntington State Park, Bethel/Redding
Huntington State Park
Sunset Hill Road
Bethel, CT 06801
(860) 424–3300

Cranberry State Park, Norwalk
Norwalk Parks and Recreation Dept.
125 East Avenue
Norwalk, CT 06851
(203) 854–7806

Mianus River Park, Greenwich/Stamford
Mianus Coalition
116B Dean Street
Stamford, CT 06902
(203) 969–1183

Tarrywile Park, Danbury
70 Southern Blvd.
Danbury, CT 06810
(203) 744–3130

New Jersey
High Point State Park, Sussex
High Point State Park
1480 State Route 23
Sussex, NJ 07461
(201) 875–4800

Ringwood State Park, Ringwood
Ringwood State Park
RD Box 1304
Ringwood, NJ 07456
(201) 962–7031

Wawayanda State Park, Highland Lakes
Wawayanda State Park
P.O. Box 198
Highland Lakes, NJ 07422
(201) 853–4462

About the Authors

Phil Harrington is a mechanical engineer at Brookhaven National Laboratories in Upton, New York, as well as a freelance writer. Over the past two decades he has biked tens of thousands of miles in and around New York City, including several "century" (100-mile) tours and other annual cycling events. He is the author of *Touring the Universe Through Binoculars, Star Ware,* and *Eclipse!* published by John Wiley and Sons, and is co-author of Globe Pequot's *Astronomy for All Ages.* He has written numerous articles for leading astronomical periodicals.

Wendy Harrington is former assistant director of nursing with the Kings Park Psychiatric Center in Kings Park, New York, as well as an aspiring author of children's books. She is a member of both Who's Who in American Nursing and Sigma Alpha Tau (nursing's national honor society). She describes herself as a casual weekend cyclist who prefers to "stop and smell the roses" rather than race past the sights.

Together with their daughter, Helen, the Harringtons spend many weekends touring the New York tristate area on two wheels.